THE Sushi Book

**By Celeste Heiter
and Photography
by Marc Schultz**

The Sushi Book
by Celeste Heiter and Photography by Marc Schultz

Cover and book design by Janet McKelpin/Dayspring Technologies, Inc.
Editing assistance provided by Robert Tompkins / Wordsdoctor Editing

For information regarding permissions, write to:
ThingsAsian Press
3230 Scott Street
San Francisco, California 94123 USA
www.thingsasianpress.com
Printed in Singapore

ISBN-10: 1-934159-00-X
ISBN-13: 978-1-934159-00-2

For Rene, with eternal love…
and thanks for all the *sushi*.

Wasabi

Tsu

Foreword

Twenty-five years ago, I worked as a waitress and bartender at the St. George Restaurant in the Napa Valley. I had only just recently moved to California from Alabama, and had never even heard of *sushi*, much less seen it or tried it. One evening, however, before we got busy with the dinner rush, I found myself in a conversation on the subject of *sushi* with Carolyn Papageorge, an eccentric and gregarious sous chef who prepared all the cold appetizers, salads and desserts for the St. George. She raved in glorious detail about the subtle flavors and sensory pleasures of this exquisite Japanese delicacy, and insisted that I try it at my earliest opportunity.

Although she couldn't remember the name of it at the time, the place she recommended was Isobune in San Francisco's Japantown, a very special type of *sushi* bar, where chefs assemble large batches at a prep station in the center of a water-filled moat, and then place individual plates of the edible treasures on a procession of little flat-bottomed wooden boats. Diners sit at a low counter on the outer side of the moat and help themselves to the plates of *sushi* as they float by. When they're finished, the waitress tallies up the bill by counting the empty plates and beverage bottles.

San Francisco is only an hour's drive south of Napa, so on my next day off, I headed to Japantown for my very first taste of *sushi*. When I arrived, however, I had no idea where I was supposed to go. The Japan Center is a huge complex with dozens of shops and Japanese restaurants, and since Carolyn couldn't remember the name or the exact location of the place she had recommended, to find it, I had to rely solely on her description. Asking directions was futile, since none of the proprietors or visitors to the Japan Center seemed to know what I was talking about. After a false start in a traditional *sushi* bar, where I was so clueless and intimidated that I didn't get any further than ordering a beer, I paid my bill and continued on my quest. Lo and Behold! Around the next corner, hidden behind a pair of low-hanging curtains, I finally stumbled upon Isobune.

Once inside, I knew I had come to the right place. The host seated me promptly at the *sushi* moat, where a *kimono*-clad waitress presented me with a steaming hot towel to cleanse my hands, along with a fragrant mug of green tea and a tiny dish of condiments. The rest was easy. There was no mystery or guesswork, since the various types of *sushi*, with both their Japanese and English names, were pictured on a laminated guide, and the prices of each type of *sushi* plate were prominently displayed on the placemats. This made it amazingly easy and fun for an absolute beginner like me to choose from among the dazzling array of treasures from the sea as they floated by on their little wooden boats.

My very first taste of *sushi* was a plate of *maguro*, two perfect slices of rosy-pink tuna, delicately draped across a pair of vinegared rice balls. That evening, I also bravely sampled flying fish roe, crab and avocado rolls, smoked salmon, and barbequed eel. I enjoyed a nice, cold Sapporo beer with my *sushi*, and ended my new dining experience with a small carafe of hot *sake*. Even after all these years, it is still the most fun, memorable, adventuresome and delightful meal I've ever had.

Since that first luscious bite of *maguro*, I have consumed untold quantities of sushi at Isobune, and have enjoyed visits to other *sushi* bars in San Francisco, as well as in Sacramento, Davis, Santa Rosa, Rohnert Park, Pinole, Bodega Bay, San Rafael, Campell, Pacifica, San Diego, Atlanta, Orlando, Las Vegas, and yes, even Tokyo.

Sushi Mambo is my favorite *sushi* bar in Napa, although ironically the owners aren't Japanese; they're two brothers from Mexico! And one of my favorite guilty pleasures, especially at times when I've been working long hours on a big deadline project, is Southern Tsunami takeout *sushi*, made fresh daily at our local gourmet grocery. I even make *sushi* at home for my son's birthday every year.

No matter how many new and exotic cuisines I try, *sushi* will always be my favorite food, and no matter how many *sushi* bars I visit, Isobune, where I had my very first taste of Japan's greatest gift to mankind, will always be my favorite restaurant in all the world. 🐟

Celeste Heiter
Napa Valley, California

Wasabi

Acknowledgments

I would like to express my gratitude to the creative individuals who participated in the production of this book for their contribution of time and talent—especially my publisher Albert Wen for his constant vision and generosity; designer Janet McKelpin for her unrivaled aesthetic gift of crafting the book you hold in your hands; photographer extraordinaire Marc Schultz for his luminous visual images; food stylist Suvisuth Chantaraprateep for his meticulous attention to detail in composing the dishes; model Zilola Mirzarasulova for looking so much more beautiful than I do while eating *sushi*; to the proprietors of Tsu, Drinking Tea Eating Rice, Wasabi, and Koi, for the generous access to their restaurants as photographic venues; to Chef Akihiro Izumi, Chef Hiroshi Kagata, Dave Lombardi, and Chef Nickolas Bovine for their time and expertise in the art of *sushi*; and to Sushi Mambo chefs José Gomez-Cazares, Francisco Gomez-Cazares and Tadashi Shirafuji for so many memorable meals and for answering my many questions. *Domo arigato gozaimashita.* 米

Table of Contents

Wasabi

Introduction

It's the 21st century. Every third car on the road is a Honda, a Nissan, a Toyota, or a Mitsubishi. And there probably isn't a household in the country that doesn't use something manufactured by Sony. The Japanese culture has produced some of the most ingenious, elegant and refined products in the history of humanity, and yet you say you've never tried its most excellent export?

Perhaps it's because you're leery of all that raw fish. Or maybe you're mystified by the names of all those unfamiliar dishes on the menu? Or could it be that you're just plain shy?

Fear not, *Sushi* Novices! Within these pages, you will find everything you need to know to help you muster the courage to walk into any *sushi* bar with your head held high, to order a meal with confidence, to savor every bite, and to relish every minute of your first visit. And even the most seasoned of *Sushi* Veterans can look forward to a trove of useful and fascinating information that will enhance your enjoyment and elevate you to the status of *Sushi* Connoisseur.

Irashai Mase! 🦐

What is *Sushi*?

In the minds of many people, *sushi* equals raw fish. However, this is merely an erroneous assumption by the uninformed and the uninitiated. Although it is true that raw fish is one of its key ingredients, the word '*sushi*' actually refers to the sticky, vinegared rice that is its essential component. And while the ultimate delicacy, several perfect slices of raw fish served all by itself without the vinegared rice, is commonly featured on most *sushi* menus, technically, it is not *sushi*, it's *sashimi*.

A little known fact among those who cringe at the mention of *sushi* is that many of the most popular items on a typical *sushi* menu aren't served raw, or they aren't even fish at all. Shrimp, crab, and eel are all cooked before serving, salmon may be lightly smoked, and many types of *sushi* are made with hen's eggs, *tofu*, and raw or pickled vegetables, not to mention the delicious soups, salads and appetizers that may accompany the meal. So, for anyone with an aversion to raw fish, and even for devout vegetarians, there are still plenty of items on the *sushi* menu to be sampled and enjoyed.

That being said, the world of *sushi* is as diverse as the millions of individuals who prepare and enjoy it. Virtually anything edible that swims, lives or grows in the sea, and even many

flora and *fauna* native to *terra firma*, have been made into
sushi. As long as it is placed on top of, or surrounded by
vinegared rice, then it's *sushi*! This leaves the subject open for
very broad and creative interpretation, and therefore, many
avant-garde *sushi* chefs offer their own signature creations
using such seemingly incongruous ingredients as cream cheese,
mayonnaise, avocado, and even beef. Yet somehow, it all works.

So, without trepidation, think beyond raw fish to the bounty of
ingredients that may be transformed by the art of *sushi* into
an endless variety of elegant edible delicacies. And trust that,
regardless of individual tastes or gastronomic aversions, there is
sure to be something on the *sushi* menu to please every palate. 🍱

Wasabi

The History of *Sushi*

The edible art of *sushi* has evolved over thousands of years. It began as a special technique for preserving raw fish, developed by the early inhabitants of the mountainous regions of Southeast Asia, especially Thailand, Laos, Myanmar and Malaysia. The earliest mention of *sushi* was found in a Chinese dictionary around 200 A.D.

The process involved packing the fish in salted rice, which produced lactic acid, a pickling agent. After several months, the rice was discarded and the fermented fish was ready to eat. Over time, however, the use of rice in the fermentation process was discontinued, and by the turn of the 19th century, this early method of *sushi* preparation had vanished altogether.

Sushi was introduced to Japan in the 7th century A.D. and evolved in the region around Lake Biwa from a somewhat different method of preparation called *narezushi*. Raw carp was alternated with layers of rice and salt in a wooden bucket, weighted with a heavy stone. The fish was allowed to ferment for several weeks, after which the stone was replaced with a light wooden cover and the fish continued to cure for months or even years before it was ready to eat.

The first mention of *narezushi* was in the *Taiho-Ritsuryo*, an early 8th century legal document that refers to *awabi* (abalone) and *igai* (mussels) being used in its preparation. Some restaurants in Japan still feature this ancient style of *sushi* made with freshwater carp, although it is very strong in flavor and for many, it is an acquired taste.

By the turn of the 16th century, the lengthy *sushi* fermentation process had been reduced to a few weeks with a method known as *nama nare*. The process still involved layering the fish with rice and salt, and weighting it with a stone. However, the *sushi* was now consumed along with the rice in a semi-fermented state. Two common types of *nama nare* were *Ayu-zushi* and *Suzume-zushi*. The former was made with a small, sweet freshwater fish called *ayu*, which was (and still is) caught using trained cormorants; the latter consisted of carp which was stuffed with cooked rice and then pressed under a stone weight.

Japan's main island of Honshu is divided into the Kanto and Kansai plains, with Tokyo and Osaka as their respective centers of commerce, and two distinct regional styles of *sushi* soon evolved from this accelerated preparation method—*Edo* style, which was developed in the ancient capital of Edo, now called Tokyo; and *Kansai* style, which was developed around the city of Osaka, an important commercial center.

In Osaka, where rice was especially abundant, *sushi* was made by filling square wooden boxes with cooked rice topped with thin slices of raw fish. The *sushi* cakes were then tightly pressed with a wooden lid and cut into bite-sized rectangles. This style of *sushi*, known as *Osaka-zushi*, is still the preferred method of preparation in the Kansai area.

Because Tokyo is located on a large bay, *Edomae-zushi* (which literally means 'in front of Tokyo' *sushi*) naturally featured an abundance of delicacies from the sea. And in the mid-17th century, Dr. Matsumoto Yoshichi, court physician of the fourth Tokugawa shogun Ietsuna, began adding rice wine vinegar to *sushi* rice. And although the basic preparation was the same, not only did the vinegar enhance the flavor of the *sushi*, it considerably reduced the fermentation time.

Nineteenth-century Edo was a bustling city, teeming with people on the go. *Sushi* as we know it today was developed in Edo in 1824 by an innovative and industrious street vendor named Yohei Hanaya. Sensing the need for food that could be quickly prepared and conveniently consumed, Hanaya hit upon the idea of serving bite-sized portions of vinegared rice topped with tiny slices of fresh raw fish. Hanaya's *sushi* stand in the Tokyo district of Ryogoku, known for its *sumo* tournaments, was an instant success, and he soon had a legion of copycat competitors all over the city who were eager to reap the rewards of this profitable new enterprise.

When the Great Kanto Earthquake of 1923 devastated the city of Tokyo, many of its *sushi* vendors returned to their rural hometowns, where they opened *sushi* stalls and introduced this edible delight to the outlying provinces of Japan. A little over twenty years later, the end of World War II resulted in the occupation of Japan by American military personnel, many of whom returned home to the U.S. with a love of *sushi*. By the 1970s, *sushi* was all the rage among the jet set and savvy city-dwellers who were always on the prowl for the latest in trendy cuisine. In the 1990s, the ubiquitous *sushi* bar began springing up in such out-of-the-way places as Omaha, Nebraska, Jackson Hole, Wyoming, Plano, Texas, and Fairbanks, Alaska.

For a cuisine, the humble beginning of which was nothing more than a means of staving off hunger throughout the lean winter months, *sushi* continues to evolve with each new interpretation, and has been elevated to one of the world's highest and most popular culinary art forms. 🦐

Wasabi

Koi

The Evolution of the *Sushi* Bar

The convention of preparing and serving *sushi* at portable stands on the streets of old Tokyo is one that lasted from the opening of Yohei Hanaya's humble establishment in 1864, to the Allied Occupation of Japan in 1945 after World War II. *Sushi* vendors vied for the most popular spots in the city, often paying a steep price for the rights to park their carts at locations with the most foot traffic.

Early *sushi* stands consisted of little more than a wheeled cart with a latticed wooden panel for the proprietor to sit behind, a roof to protect him from the elements, a panel of short curtains called *noren*, and a small counter for bowls of soy sauce and pickled ginger. Some stands also featured a raised *tatami* mat, which served as a seating area for patrons.

Each evening, the proprietor of the *sushi* stand would wheel his cart into place, hang out his *noren* curtains, and commence with the preparation of *sushi* from a wooden box of fresh fish and a wooden vat of vinegared rice, which he brought from home. A bucket of water to rinse his sticky hands was begged or borrowed from nearby homes or businesses.

Nightlife in Edo included performances of *Kabuki* Theater, and visits to public baths or *geisha* houses. A stop-off at a *sushi* stand along the way to and from was all part of an evening's entertainment.

Those *sushi* vendors who could not afford to open a sidewalk stand could still make a handsome living selling pre-made *sushi* carried in boxes strapped to their backs. Those *sushi* vendors who fared well in their enterprise often went on to open permanent *sushi* shops in the most fashionable districts of the city.

When the people of Japan rebuilt the city of Tokyo after the Great Kanto Earthquake of 1923, many *sushi* vendors chose to establish fixed locations. Sometimes they parked the original cart in front of the shop, where patrons could still enjoy their *sushi* outdoors. Inside, chairs were provided for patrons waiting for take-out *sushi*, and those who chose to eat on the premises would stand at the counter, where they could dip the *sushi* in common bowls of soy sauce and share a dish of pickled ginger.

During the Allied Occupation, *sushi* vendors were prohibited from peddling their fare on the streets of Tokyo. Nevertheless, the Japanese people continued to enjoy *sushi* at the hundreds of restaurants that sprang up all over the city.

Modern technology brought about yet another *sushi* innovation called *kaiten-zushi*, a kind of inexpensive *sushi* diner in which patrons sit at a counter, where a variety of individual plates of *sushi* pass by on a circular conveyor belt in front of them. Of course, modern-day Tokyo now features some of the finest and most exclusive *sushi* restaurants in the world, as does virtually every cosmopolitan city in nearly every country on the planet.

Yohei Hanaya: The Father of Modern *Sushi*

Born in 1799 in the Echizen region of Japan, now known as Fukui Prefecture, Yohei Hanaya went to Edo, now the city of Tokyo, when he was nine years old to apprentice as a rice broker in the district of Ryogoku. In 1824, Yohei Hanaya hit upon the idea of selling bite-sized *nigiri sushi* from a sidewalk stand to busy people on the go. Hanaya's *sushi* stand was an overnight success and soon became known throughout the city. Yohei Hanaya's *sushi* stand survived in the same spot in Ryogoku for many generations thereafter, until it finally closed in 1932 after 108 years in business. 🦀

Sushi in Art History

Around the same time that Yohei Hanaya opened his *sushi* stand in the Edo district of Ryogoku, the Japanese art of painting and woodblock printmaking known as *Ukiyo-e* had reached its zenith. Many *Ukiyo-e* scenes depict aristocratic ladies and gentlemen, as well as renowned *Kabuki* performers, enjoying *sushi* in the elegant 'floating world' of the Edo Period.

Mitate Genji Hana No En
by Kuniyoshi (1797-1862)

Japanese works of art known as *mitate-e* are scenes from historical events or classic works of literature placed in a contemporary setting, often with a visual pun implied. *Gengi Monogatari* is Japan's oldest and most renowned literary work. Written in the 11th century by Lady Murasaki Shikibu, daughter of the governor of a province belonging to the Fujiwara family, this epic tale chronicles the romantic escapades of playboy Prince Genji. *Mitate Genji Hana No En* (Genji's Flower Garden) features allusions to the tale of Genji at a traditional *O-hanami* party, when friends gather to celebrate the ephemeral beauty of the cherry blossoms, while sharing an elegant repast of *sushi* and *sake*.

Tohto Koumei Kaiseki-zukushi
by Utagawa Toyokuni III and Ando Hiroshige

Another theme typical of *mitate-e* prints is that of *Kabuki* actors, often idealized by wealthy patrons in commissioned works featuring the actors in classical roles, starring with actors whom they never actually met onstage, in plays that were composed and staged long after they had died.

One such classic tale is that of *Yoshitsune Senbon-Zakura* (Yoshitsune and the Thousand Cherry Trees), the story of a fugitive *samurai* warrior during a longstanding feud between the Genji and Heike clans of the Minamoto and Taira families. Originally composed by Takeda Izumo II, Miyoshi Shôraku, and Namiki Sôsuke as a *Bunraku* puppet play in 1747, due to its popularity, it was immediately adapted for performance in the *Kabuki* Theater. Act 3, Scene 2, takes place at a *sushi* shop, in a plot twist involving three wooden *sushi* buckets, one containing a severed head, another a stash of stolen money.

In a series of collaborations by famed *Ukiyo-e* artists Utagawa Toyokuni III and Ando Hiroshige, published by Fujikei Printing House in 1852, Toyokuni rendered portraits of *Kabuki* actors, and Hiroshige provided restaurant-themed backgrounds. One woodblock print in the series features the *sushi* restaurant Matsu no Sushi in the Heizaemon district of *Edo* (the first restaurant ever to serve *nigiri sushi* in old Tokyo) with a young woman named Osato in the role of the heroine in the aforementioned story *Yoshitsune Senbon-Zakura*. Hiroshige's background features fan-shaped insets with *sushi bento* boxes and serving dishes, and the restaurant name, Matsu no Sushi, written in elegant calligraphy. The *mitate-e* surprise is that the print was created at a time when women were prohibited from performing onstage, and the young woman featured is the daughter of Yasuke, the owner of a *sushi* shop called Tsurube-zushi at Yoshino in the province of Nara. In its day, this *Ukiyo-e* print was so highly recognized that the restaurant owner's name, Yasuke, became synonymous with *sushi*.

Another print in the Toyokuni-Hiroshige series features the restaurant En-en Tei in the Tokyo district of Sanya-Tanaka, now known as Shin-Yoshiwara. Hiroshige's background includes one inset of a landscape with swallows flying over a marsh, and another of a tub filled with *nigiri sushi* topped with tuna, mackerel, sea bream and gizzard shad. The play alluded to by the *Kabuki* actor's portrait is the classic tale of *Fuwa*, in which *samurai* rivals Fuwa Banzaemon and Nagoya Sanza vie for the affection of the Lady Katsuragi. The climactic moment of the play comes when their sheathed swords accidentally touch as the two pass each other on a crowded street, resulting in a near-fatal duel, until the Lady Katsuragi intervenes. The two characters can be distinguished by the decorative motifs on each *samurai's kimono*. Fuwa's features clouds and lightning, while Sanza's is decorated with swallows and rain. The *mitate-e* elements in the woodblock print are the umbrellas, symbolizing rain on the actor's *kimono*, and a visual play on words with the name of the restaurant, EnenTei, which means Swallow-Swallow Restaurant.

Sushi Fukumoto and Shijaku-wage
By Hasegawa Sadanobu

This colorful *Ukiyo-e* print from a series featuring well known Osaka restaurants and beautiful women with elaborate hair styles, pays homage to *Fukomoto-zushi*, known for a *sushi* dish called *kokera-zushi*, made with abalone, sea bream and egg omelet. The print depicts a beautiful young woman in an elegant floral *kimono* beneath a fan-shaped inset of the Osaka-style *hako-zushi*, a regional specialty made by pressing rice into the bottom of a wooden box and topping it with thin slices of fish. The pressed sushi cake is then cut into bite-sized pieces.

Shima-zoroi On'na-benkei (Matsuno-zushi)
By Utagawa Yoshikuni

This classic *Ukiyo-e* print features a *kimono*-clad woman holding a wooden box labeled *Matsuno-zushi*, the name of a popular *sushi* establishment of the day. With the other hand, she is offering a plate of *futomaki* and *maguro nigiri* to her eager child.

Atake Matsuga-zushi
By Utagawa Toyokuni III

Three Japanese beauties pass each other on the street in front
of Matsu no Sushi, one of Edo's finest *sushi* shops, located at
Ataka in the Fukagawa district. The woman to the far left holds
a wooden tub filled with the house specialty, mackerel *sushi*,
an expensive seasonal delicacy.

Tohto Meisho Takanawa Nijyuu-rokuya-machi Yuukyou-no-zu
(Feast in Waiting for the Moon at Takanawa, Edo on the
Twenty-sixth Night)
By Ando Hiroshige (From the series Famous Places in Edo)

This triptych work depicts a bustling marketplace along the
shores of the harbor at Takanawa. It is lined with vendors offering
a tempting array of edible street fare, including grilled squid,
tempura, *soba* noodles, *gyoza* dumplings, and mackerel *sushi*,
at a stand that can easily be identified by the huge characters
'su-shi' on the side. The occasion is a festival to celebrate the
rising of the crescent moon on July 26. 🍣

The Art of *Sushi*

The Philosophy

The beauty of Japanese cuisine, especially *sushi*, is its *Zen*-like simplicity. No fussy sauces, no overwrought concoctions, no pretentious contrivances. Just the freshest seasonal ingredients harmoniously combined to please the eye as well as the palate. But beyond the quality of the ingredients and their preparation is an inherent attitude of reverence, respect, gratitude, and a sense of *joie de vie* toward food, and toward life itself. When it comes to *sushi*, think Clean, Fresh, Simple, Alive!

The Preparation

Though endlessly varied, the essence of *sushi* lies in its simplicity. What could be more perfect than a single slice of raw fish atop a snowy-white oval of vinegared rice? And even when the preparation of *sushi* entails more complex combinations of ingredients, simplicity and harmony of flavor, color, shape and texture are the key components.

Based upon the concept that all nature's bounty is perfect as is, the goal of the *sushi* chef is not intended to bend the ingredients to his will, but rather to enhance the flavors and textures of the food without robbing it of its natural beauty. Therefore, cooking, if any, is minimal. Sauces and other composed dishes rarely contain more than three or four ingredients. And all components are mindfully balanced so that no single element overpowers the others.

As with many other traditional Japanese arts, such as flower arranging or the tea ceremony, the arrangement of food is a highly refined art called *moritsuke*, of which there are five basic styles, depending upon the food being prepared and the dishes upon which it is served. The five basic styles are *hiramori*, which means flat; *yamamori*, which means mounded; *sugimori*, which means slanting; *ayamori*, which means overlapping; and *yose-mori*, which means gathered.

The Presentation

The art of Japanese tableware began thousands of years ago and includes ceramic, porcelain, lacquerware, metal, wood, and bamboo. And much like the food served upon it, the design of Japanese dishes is based upon nature and simplicity. Its lines are clean, its shapes functional. Decorative motifs are borrowed from nature, and colors are subtle and harmonious.

The dishes upon which *sushi* is served are as much an integral part of the experience as the food itself, and garnishes are often used to create the illusion of the food in its natural setting. The arrangement of *sushi* on the plate is never busy or crowded, and the garnish never overwrought. *Sushi* is modestly arranged on plates, leaving plenty of unfilled space so that the aesthetic elements of the dish may be appreciated along with the beauty of the *sushi* itself. 🍵

Wasabi

Tsu

Treasures from the Sea

The island nation of Japan is surrounded by vast expanses of water, including the Pacific Ocean, known in Japan as *Taiheiyo*, to the east and south; the Sea of Japan, known as *Nihon Kai*, to the west; the Sea of Okhotsk, known as *Ohotuku Kai*, to the north; and an inland sea known as *Setonaikai*, which separates the islands of Honshu, Kyushu, and Shikoku. Japan's 18,000 mile (28,968 km) coastline forms thousands of quiet bays and inlets, and the steep volcanic terrain is traversed by hundreds of streams and rivers. So it goes without saying that the variety and abundance of marine life available for the preparation of *sushi* is virtually endless.

The Stars of the Show

For the art of *sushi*, there are hundreds of fish, shellfish, and other marine creatures, as well as a bounty of seaweed, pickles, fresh vegetables and other assorted ingredients that either complement or stand on their own. Yet it seems no matter where you go, about a dozen standard favorites always seem to steal the show.

Tuna is by far the most popular and versatile of the *sushi* divas, with appearances by yellowtail, salmon, shrimp, crab, squid, octopus, clams, eel, snapper, and mackerel as the supporting cast. Of course, this short list doesn't even begin to address local and seasonal favorites, such as roe and other exotica, or the endless variety of combined ingredients that may be rolled into *sushi maki*.

All About Tuna

Known in Japanese as *maguro*, tuna is the most craved and coveted fish for *sushi*. However, *maguro* is only the collective name for a wide sub-category of species, sizes, grades, and cuts.

Bluefin is the preferred tuna for *sushi*. Known in scientific terms as *Thunnus thynnus*, in Japan, bluefin tuna is commonly referred to as *hon-maguro, kuro-maguro,* and *shibi-maguro.* And although they range in size from 20 to 1500 lbs. (9 to 680 kg.), and up to 15 ft. (4.6 m.) or more in length, those categorized as *nakaboshi*, weighing between 300 and 500 lbs. (136 and 227 kg.) are ideal. Anything smaller may lack color and flavor, while the flavor of the larger fish may be gamey and overpowering. Fresh bluefin tuna is best enjoyed in season, which is during the summer in the U.S., and during the winter months in Japan.

A sub-species of bluefin tuna that may find its way to your local *sushi* bar is *minami maguro* (southern bluefin). However, since it is native to the Indian Ocean, *minami maguro* must be frozen for shipping to distant markets, which may affect the flavor and texture of its dark, rich meat.

Yellowfin tuna, *Thunnus albacares*, known also as *ahi* and commonly served as *sushi*, is a much smaller variety, weighing up to only 300 lbs. (135 kg.). Yellowfin is somewhat milder in flavor and lighter in color than its bluefinned cousin, and can often be recognized by a network of fine purplish veins that run throughout its meat. Known in Japan as *kihada* or *kiwada*, yellowfin tuna is best enjoyed during the winter months and into early spring in the U.S., where it is the most economical, abundant, and popular variety of tuna for *sushi*.

Shiro Maguro, which translates as 'white tuna,' is the same albacore you will find in the higher priced cans of tuna at the supermarket. Known also as *binnaga*, and scientifically as *Thunnus alalunga*, reaching a maximum weight of only about 40 lbs. (18 kg.), *shiro maguro* is peachy or rosy in color when served raw as *sushi*, although exposure to air quickly renders its delicate, translucent flesh darker and more opaque. As a result, some *sushi* chefs serve *shiro maguro* lightly seared on the outside. The fatty underbelly of *shiro maguro* is called *binjo*.

If the tuna you order at a *sushi* bar is an unnaturally brilliant shade of red or hot pink, chances are it was imported from the Philippines. This low-grade tuna may have been preserved by a smoking process that leaves no telltale aroma or flavor, but dramatically affects the color of the meat. Another variety to be avoided for the preparation of *sushi* is big-eye tuna. Known in the scientific world as *Thunnus obesus*, and in Japanese as *mebachi*, the meat of the big-eye tuna is extremely oily and gamey, especially near the skin. Not the best choice for *sushi*.

Making the Cut

After your first few visits to a *sushi* bar, you may begin to notice subtle variations in the appearance of tuna from one piece to the next. This is because several distinctive species of tuna are used for *sushi*, and as with any other type of meat such as beef or lamb, the various cuts of tuna also differ in appearance.

Once the head and tail have been removed, and the entrails eviscerated, the meat of the tuna is filleted away from the bones on each side from dorsal fin to belly. The red meat along the spine from the inner center of the body and upper back is called *akami*; meat from the broad outer side near the skin is called *chu-toro*; and meat from the underbelly is called *toro*.

Among the various cuts of tuna, the leaner the meat, the deeper the color. The leanest cuts come from the meat surrounding the spine, whereas the belly meat is much higher in fat content and therefore lighter in color. Much like filet mignon, which runs along the spine of a cow, the *akami* tuna with the finest texture and the fewest muscular striations comes from near the spine and is the tenderest; the meat near the tail of the fish, which is highly developed for swimming, is more muscular and therefore less tender.

Chu means middle or central, and the *chu-toro* cut of the tuna comes from the broad side of the fish near the skin. Because it surrounds the deep red *akami* section and also borders the *toro* section, *chu-toro* sometimes has a gradient color that ranges from light pink to pale red.

Toro cut from the belly of the tuna is graded according to its fat content, and the choicest cuts of *toro* are pale, tender and buttery in texture with a subtle, naturally smoky flavor. The *toro* section of the tuna is further divided into two sections—the *shimofuri* section just below the head, and the *dandara* section that runs along the remainder of the lower belly all the way to the tail. Cuts made from the *shimofuri* section are fleshy-pink and marbled with a net-like pattern, while the *dandara* cuts are the most fatty of all. *Toro* is among the rarest and most prized of all *sushi* delicacies, and a pair of *o-toro nigiri* at the average neighborhood *sushi* bar may be priced at upwards of $20, and even higher at more exclusive establishments.

Special Names for the Various Cuts of Tuna
akami – lean red tuna filet
chu-toro – semi-fatty side meat
dandara – fatty underbelly meat from center section to tail
hoho niku – cheek

kama toro – meat between the gill and pectoral fin
kawagishi – meat near the skin
maguro – lean meat near the spine
naka ochi – meat near the rib
onomi – tail meat
shimofuri – fatty underbelly meat just below the head
tenmi – head
toro – fatty underbelly meat

How Fresh is It?

Much like warm-blooded meats such as beef or pork, within a
few hours after a fish is caught, if it is not consumed immediately,
it will undergo the process of *rigor mortis*, in which blood
circulation ceases, causing muscular proteins to coagulate.
Depending upon the type of fish and the way in which it is
handled, this stiffening and aging of the flesh can last from a
few hours to several days. And once *rigor mortis* sets in, the
fish should not be eaten until the process is complete and the
meat becomes soft and flexible again. Fish consumed immediately
after it is caught has a distinctively wild, gamey flavor, especially
in the larger types.

Fresh, properly aged tuna should be translucent, with a
healthy pink to deep red color, odorless and have a mild to
rich flavor. Fish that looks cloudy or murky, has a fishy odor
and a questionable taste is obviously beyond its prime and
should be avoided.

From Ocean to Market to Plate

Once the tuna has been caught, exsanguinated, iced, shipped,
eviscerated, skinned and filleted, the sides of meat are divided
lengthwise from head to tail and sold in blocks called *cho*,
which are either the lean, upper *akami* section, or the fatty,
lower toro section. Due to the curvature of the body, a *cho* is

somewhat triangular in shape, like one-quarter of an oval, and must be trimmed to form the rectangular blocks from which individual portions of *nigiri sushi* are sliced. The trimmings are used for making *tekka maki*, spicy tuna rolls, and other specialties that do not require the bits of tuna to be perfectly shaped.

Fresh tuna labeled '*sushi* grade' means that it is extremely high in quality, has been shipped and handled properly, has been kept separate from other types of fish, is free of parasites, and is therefore safe to eat raw.

High quality tuna also freezes well, and previously frozen tuna is perfectly safe to use for *sushi*, provided it has been properly handled. In fact, much of the tuna sold in retail fish markets arrives frozen, and is thawed for display at the seafood counter. However, the quality varies greatly, and therefore *sushi*-grade tuna for home consumption should only be purchased from a trusted fish merchant. Pre-packaged tuna on display at the supermarket, no matter how fresh and tempting it may look, is not typically '*sushi* grade' and is therefore unsafe to eat raw.

Yellowtail

Typically listed on *sushi* menus as *hamachi*, yellowtail or amberjack is the collective name for several species of *Seriola*, including *Seriola quinqueradiata* from Japan, *Seriola dorsalis* from California, and *Seriola grandis* from Australia. Yellowtail is a cylindrical fish with a gold stripe that runs lengthwise along its body to the yellow tail that inspires its name.

Much smaller than most varieties of tuna, yellowtail typically reaches an average length of only 3 ft. (1 m.), and a maximum weight of about 30 lbs. (14 kg.), although the Australian variety tends to be somewhat larger. However, yellowtail is also available in much smaller sizes, each with its own name. The smallest fry are called *mojako*, fingerlings are called *wakashi*, adolescent yellowtail are called *inada*, young adults are called *warasa*, and fully grown yellowtail are called *buri*.

There are several other species related to the yellowtail, including *hiramasa*, a larger, gold-striped amberjack, *Seriola lalandi*, with lean, firm flesh and a mild flavor; *kanpachi*, *Seriola rivoliana*, a blue-purple fish with a deep gold stripe, very lean flesh and somewhat richer flavor; and *shima aji*, a plump silver fish with the characteristic yellow stripe and tail, and slightly darker flesh with a rind of reddish meat near the skin.

Yellowtail labeled *hamachi* are actually raised in commercial fish hatcheries in Japan, where they are specially bred and fed to enhance the buttery tenderness of the meat. *Hamachi* are somewhat smaller than their ocean-going cousins, only reaching about 2 ft. (.6 m.) in length and 20 lbs. (9 kg.) in weight before they are harvested at about a year old.

The flesh of the yellowtail is creamy in taste, texture, and color, with a darker, more flavorful band of meat near the bone. And much like tuna, the underbelly of *hamachi*, called *sunazuri*, is even more succulent.

Salmon

Salmon are divided into two categories: Pacific and Atlantic. Pacific salmon are further divided into seven distinct species: chinook, also known as king salmon; sockeye, also known as red salmon; coho, also known as silver salmon; chum, also known as dog salmon; pink, also known as humpback salmon; and two Asian varieties: *masu*, also known as *yamame*; and *amago*, also known as *biwamasu*, all of which die shortly after spawning.

Chinook, sockeye and coho are the Pacific varieties most commonly found in fish markets. Chinook is the rarest and largest, averaging 15 to 40 lbs. (7 to 18 kg.), with brilliant orange flesh, high fat content, and rich, buttery texture. Sockeye salmon is smaller and oilier than chinook, and is a popular choice for *sushi* and *sashimi*. Coho salmon has pink or red-orange flesh, which is leaner and milder in flavor than chinook and sockeye.

Pacific salmon are in season from May through September, with most of the catch coming from Alaskan waters, since they are on the endangered list in Washington, Oregon, and Northern California

There is only one species of Atlantic salmon, which, unlike Pacific salmon, often survives spawning. However, due to overfishing, Atlantic salmon for human consumption are mostly raised in commercial hatcheries and offshore pens in Canada, Chile, Great Britain, Iceland, Ireland, and Norway, averaging about 10 lbs. (4.5 kg.) when harvested. The flesh of Atlantic salmon is bright pink and higher in fat content than Pacific salmon.

Although salmon makes some of the most excellent *nigiri sushi* and *sushi maki*, not all salmon is suitable for *sushi*. Salmon is an ocean-going fish that traverses the coastal waters between salty and fresh for its annual trip upstream to spawn, and the time the fish spend in fresh water can leave them infested with harmful parasites, mainly sea lice, worms, and the eggs they leave behind as they burrow through the flesh. Commercially cultivated Atlantic salmon have a much lower likelihood of common parasites, and are therefore the safest to use for *sushi*.

To prepare wild salmon for safe consumption as *sushi*, the meat must undergo one or more purification techniques. One method is freezing at 32°F (0°C) for 72 hours, a commercial process that is not possible with ordinary household freezers. Hard freezing kills any parasites that may have burrowed into the flesh, rendering them harmless to humans.

Another method, although not as effective as freezing, is to cover the salmon filets with the skin still intact in a layer of coarse salt crystals and allow the meat to cure for an hour or more, which weakens but does not always kill the parasites. After curing, the salt is rinsed away, leaving the salmon somewhat firmer and moderately safer to eat.

A third method is a rice vinegar or rice wine marinade for up to an hour, which weakens or destroys any parasites in the flesh. However, much like the salt cure, this method is not as effective as a hard freeze, and changes the color, texture and flavor of the fish.

Some *sushi* chefs take extra precaution by using all three methods: they buy fresh, farm-raised salmon, cure it in salt, marinate it in vinegar, and freeze it for 72 hours to produce the safest possible 'raw' salmon for *sushi*.

And finally, smoking is an effective method of destroying parasites in salmon, although it dramatically alters the flavor and texture of the meat for a completely different salmon *sushi* experience.

Shrimp

Known in Japanese as *ebi*, shrimp is one of the most familiar and popular items on any *sushi* menu. There are 342 edible species of shrimp, 109 of which are warm-water *Penaeid* shrimp, and 34 species are cold-water *Pandalid* shrimp. And although the cold-water variety are deep sea creatures that do not ingest mud and sand with their food, leaving their veins cleaner than those of warm-water shrimp, the warm-water variety are by far the most popular shrimp for *sushi*.

More than a million tons of shrimp are commercially grown worldwide each year, with the most popular species being black tiger shrimp, *Penaeus monodon* at 61%, with Western white shrimp, *Penaeus vannamei*, following a distant second at 15%. Thailand is the top exporter of shrimp to the U.S. market, along with other major suppliers such as Ecuador, Mexico, China, and India.

The most commonly served variety of *sushi* shrimp is called *kuruma ebi*, meaning 'wheel shrimp' in Japanese. Because they are susceptible to parasites, they are always served cooked. To prepare them for *nigiri sushi*, the shrimp are peeled with the tails left intact, after which the chef runs a bamboo skewer along the length of the body to keep them from curling when they are immersed in boiling salted water. Once cooked, the now pink-and-white-striped shrimp are butterflied with a sharp knife, laid flat over pads of vinegared rice, and served in pairs.

One delicate and delicious exception to boiled *ebi* is another variety of *sushi* called *ama ebi*, sweet shrimp, which is peeled, butterflied and served raw. This variety comes from cold, deep Northern waters on the periphery of the Arctic Circle, where there is little or no danger of parasites, and therefore *ama ebi* are safe to eat raw. The ultimate rarity is the female *ama ebi* with her roe still intact. As an added bonus, many *sushi* bars serve each pair of *ama ebi* alongside their own crispy, deep-fried heads, but with eyes, innards and tentacles intact, which may be eaten in their entirety, much like soft-shelled crabs.

Yet another even less common variety of shrimp *sushi* is *shako*, also known as mantis shrimp. These somewhat more rugged-looking relatives of the common shrimp are peeled, boiled, brushed with a thick, sweetened soy sauce and served as *nigiri sushi*.

Crab

Crab for *sushi* comes in many varieties, including Alaskan king crab, Dungeness crab, snow crab, blue crab, and an especially popular delicacy, soft-shelled crab. The Alaskan king crab is highly favored for *sushi*, not only for the taste of its meat, but also for its size and abundance. Crab for *sushi* is always cooked before serving, and is frequently shipped already cooked and frozen for commercial distribution.

The meat of the Alaskan king crab is creamy white, and develops a rosy blush when cooked. Their enormous legs and claws yield long segments of firm flesh, while their bodies produce generous chunks of lump crabmeat suitable for a variety of *makizushi* combinations. Unfortunately, some of its flavor is lost in the freezing process, and therefore crab of any kind is best when served fresh.

For the cultivation of soft-shelled crabs, Asian swimming crabs are gathered from the sea, especially in the waters surrounding Vietnam. They are held in special tanks until they are ready to molt, and are harvested, cleaned and packaged for shipping within hours or even minutes of shedding their shells. To prepare for *sushi*, soft-shelled crabs are deep-fried, and either served on their own to be consumed shell and all, or deconstructed and rolled into *makizushi*.

One last variety of crab worth mentioning, if only for its widespread use, is imitation crab, a processed fish paste, shaped and colored to resemble Alaskan king crab legs. It is readily available at almost any supermarket, and many *sushi* bars serve it without apology in California rolls, seafood *gunkanmaki*, and even as *nigiri sushi*.

Sometimes called 'krab' to distinguish it from the real thing, imitation crab is most commonly made from an abundant and nearly flavorless fish called Alaska pollock. In a process that has its origins in a 16th century Japanese technique for making a type of fish cake called *kamaboko*, imitation crab is made by cleaning, de-boning and washing the filleted pollack, which is then minced into a fine paste called *surimi*. Excess water is removed and the mixture is flash-frozen to -4°F (-20°C) until time for shaping and coloring, when the *surimi* is thawed to 25°F (-4°C) and shaved into large flakes. The semi-frozen *surimi* flakes are then blended together in a stone grinder with additives such as sugar and sorbitol to prevent breakdown during freezing; starch, vegetable oil and egg whites to enhance texture; natural crab by-products and artificial flavorings designed to mimic the taste of real crabmeat; and seasonings such as MSG and rice wine to enhance flavor.

When the recipe is complete, the *surimi* is transferred to a machine that presses the paste into thin, smooth sheets about 10 in. (25 cm.) wide. The sheets are then cooked and shredded with steel rollers into tiny ribbons to further mimic the appearance of real crabmeat. The sheets of strands are rolled into cylindrical ropes, and artificially colored in shades of red, orange, and pink, using carmine, caramel, paprika, and annatto. Next, the imitation crab is cut into uniform lengths, vacuum packed and pasteurized in a steam cooker to prevent bacteria and extend shelf life.

All that being said, since it is the product of such an elaborate and intensive manufacturing process, one can't help but wonder how imitation crab can be sold at such economical prices.

Squid

Squid is one of the most abundant and popular species of marine life on the planet. There are nearly 500 different types of squid, ranging in size from 1 in. (2.5 cm.) to more than 50 ft. (15 m.) in length.

Squid are cephalopods, which means 'head foot,' and have ten tentacles surrounding a mouth at the lower end of a tube-shaped body, with a pair of triangular fins on either side at the other end. Squid maneuver about by contracting the cylindrical mantle to expel water, and two of their tentacles can be used to seize prey, which they tear apart with a beak-like feature. When threatened, they discharge a sudden cloud of dark fluid to obscure them from their predators as they escape. Some squid are chromataphores, which means that they can change color according to their surroundings as a camouflage, while others have luminescent organs.

In the U.S., the common squid is native to the Atlantic Ocean, from Maine to the Carolinas. They are also abundant in the Mediterranean Sea, and the waters surrounding the Asian continent.

On Italian menus, this tasty cephalopod is called *calamari*, and is usually battered, deep-fried, and served with a creamy dipping sauce, or marinated raw in a citrus vinaigrette. On a *sushi* menu, however, squid is called *ika*, and its presentation varies from the pristine perfection of a single slice, blanched and served *nigiri*-style atop a pad of vinegared rice with a single *shiso* leaf, to marinated concoctions with other ingredients, among them quail egg, fermented soybeans called *natto*, spicy cod roe called *mentaiko*, and *shiokara*, squid intestines preserved in salt. In its *nigiri* form, squid is very mild in flavor and somewhat rubbery and chewy in texture.

Octopus

The eight-tentacled cephalopod known as the octopus is one of the most colorful and easily identifiable items in any *sushi* bar. When blanched, its skin and suction cups turn a lovely shade of rosy purple, while the inner flesh remains snow white. In Japanese, octopus is called *tako*, and for *nigiri sushi*, the blanched tentacles of the octopus are sliced thin and scored on the underside to keep them from curling. Octopus is also frequently served as an appetizer called *sunomono*, in a light marinade of sesame oil and rice wine vinegar with fresh cucumber. The flavor of octopus is quite mild, although the texture is somewhat chewy and rubbery.

Although they are also native to Japan, octopus for *sushi* now come mainly from the waters around the continent of Africa, and average about 4 to 5 lbs. (1.8 to 2.3 kg.) each, with a single tentacle weighing about .5 lbs. (.2 kg.). Tiny baby octopus is served whole in some sushi bars.

In their natural habitat, the octopus is monogamous, sometimes poisonous, and carnivorous, using its tentacles to grasp its prey, and even to crack shellfish open with rocks.

Clams

With the exception of the seemingly endless varieties of fish, perhaps one of the most widely varied items on any *sushi* menu is the clam. Those preferred for *sushi* include *hokkigai*, the red-tipped surf clam; *akagai*, the red clam also known as ark shell; *bakagai*, the round clam; *aoyagi*, the surf clam; *asari*, the short-necked clam; *torigai*, the cockle; and *mirugai*, the giant horseneck clam.

Clams for *sushi* are frequently served raw, although blanching brings out the color and enhances texture of some varieties, which may be chewy or rubbery. Smaller clams are served whole, while the horseneck clam, also known as the geoduck, an oceanic oddity that resembles a certain part of the male anatomy that shall remain nameless, is sliced into bite-sized pieces for *nigiri sushi*. Various types of clams may also be minced into tiny bits and mixed with other ingredients for *gun-kan maki*.

Eel

There are two varieties of this snake-like creature: freshwater eel, called *unagi*, and ocean-going eel, called *anago*, both of which are usually steamed and then broiled or grilled, with a sweet soy glaze called *tsume*. This method of preparation renders the skin of the eel crispy and flavorful, while the flesh remains tender. Eel has a surprisingly mild flavor and fine texture, and is especially delicious prepared in this way, but it is never served raw. *Unagi* and *anago* may be prepared either as *nigiri* or *makizushi*, and are sometimes sprinkled with sesame seeds.

Unagi is a summertime favorite in Japan, with entire restaurants devoted solely to its preparation. The Japanese people believe that *unagi* promotes health and stamina, and some even consider it an aphrodisiac that enhances male virility. Although freshwater *unagi* is the type most frequently ordered in American *sushi* bars, the Japanese prefer the salt-water *anago* for *sushi*.

As with most other types of seafood, the most flavorful are those caught in the wild, however, eel farms produce much of the *unagi* served in *sushi* bars. Some restaurants even keep tanks of live eels to ensure the ultimate in *unagi* freshness.

Snapper

In *sushi* bars outside Japan, red snapper is the closest most *sushi* bars come to the highly coveted sea bream from the Seto Inland Sea that separates the Japanese island of Honshu from its smaller neighbors, Kyushu and Shikoku. On a *sushi* menu, both snapper and sea bream are called *tai*, however, only the Japanese variety is a popular choice for celebrations since its name also means 'congratulations.' Nevertheless, red snapper makes excellent *sushi*, and can be identified by its translucent flesh, tinged at the edges with a hint of bright red. *Tai* may also be served slightly blanched with a sliver of the skin still intact.

Mackerel

One of the most flavorful fish on any *sushi* menu is mackerel. With its deep amber flesh and pewter-colored skin, *saba*, as it is called in Japanese, is easily recognizable. For a fresh catch, mackerel is a winter fish in Japan, and a summer seasonal in the U.S. But because it spoils easily, mackerel is usually cured in salt and marinated in rice vinegar before slicing for *nigiri sushi*. 🦐

Styles and Types of *Sushi*

Sashimi

The simplest of all Japanese dishes, *sashimi* is several perfect slices of the very freshest raw fish, garnished with a chiffonade of *daikon* radish. Favorite varieties of fish for *sashimi* are tuna, yellowtail, snapper, and salmon. For the more adventurous diners, the potentially deadly blowfish called *fugu* is a popular delicacy, and even *kujira*, the raw flesh of the whale!

Nigiri sushi

Served in pairs, this style of *sushi* consists of slices of raw fish or pieces of other types of seafood, placed atop oblong balls of vinegared rice. It is also called *Edo-mae sushi*, which literally means 'in front of Edo,' the name of old Tokyo.

Makizushi

This variety of *sushi* is composed of vinegared rice and bits of fish or seafood, wrapped cigar-style in a sheet of toasted seaweed paper called *nori*, and sliced into six bite-sized pieces.

Gunkan

Its name means 'battleship,' and *gunkan sushi* is another type of *nori* roll, in which the narrow strip of seaweed paper extends slightly beyond the top of the ball of vinegared rice, creating a shallow niche to hold a small serving of a soft ingredient such as fish roe, sea urchin, or minced shellfish.

Futomaki
Much like *maki* rolls, *futomaki* is an oversized *nori* roll, filled with a colorful assortment of rice, cucumber, red ginger, pink fish cake, dried gourd, pickled yellow radish, and egg omelet. When sliced, the colorful ingredients inside form an attractive pattern in the center of each piece.

Temaki
Te means 'hand,' and *temaki* is composed of any of the same ingredients as those used to form *maki* rolls, but instead of being snugly rolled into long cylinders, the filling is wrapped in a loosely filled cone of *nori*.

Chirashi
Its name means 'scattered,' and *chirashi* is a variety of any of the ingredients typical used for *sushi*, but instead of being fashioned into bite-sized bits, the pieces of fish and seafood are informally arranged atop a bowl of vinegared rice.

Inarizushi
Pouches of deep-fried *tofu* filled with vinegared rice and other ingredients, such as pickles and sour plums, form this type of *sushi*.

Wasabi

Wasabi

The Elements of *Sushi*

Rice

Contrary to popular belief, it's not the raw fish, but rather the vinegared rice called *sushi meishi* that is the heart and soul of *sushi*. Rice worthy of *sushi* must be perfect in flavor, texture, and appearance. The type of rice used is crucial, and therefore not every variety or brand of rice is suitable for *sushi*. High quality, polished, short-grained rice is ideal, since its pearly white grains are high in starch content and stick together when cooked. Medium-grained rice may also be used, although it is somewhat lower in starch. Long-grained rice is not suitable, since it lacks the starch to stick together enough to form the hand-sculpted rice pads and rolls without falling apart.

Once cooked, the rice is transferred to a large, shallow, wooden tub called a *hangiri*, and is dressed with a mild, aromatic rice vinegar called *su*, sweetened with sugar and then seasoned with a little salt. As it cools in the *hangiri*, the rice is fanned with a flat paper fan called an *uchiwa*, as it is lightly sprinkled with the vinegar dressing, and mixed with a small wooden paddle called a *shamoji*.

Some *sushi meishi* recipes call for a small piece of *kombu* kelp in the cooking water, and some even include a splash of *sake*. Each *sushi* chef has his own personal recipe, technique, and ritual for preparing the rice, which gives his *sushi* its uniquely subtle flavor.

Nori

Nori is an edible seaweed paper made from a variety of algae called *Porphyra*, also called laver. Once it has been harvested from the sea, the algae is pulverized and laid out in thin sheets to dry. It is then cut into uniform squares and packaged for commercial distribution. Japan once produced enough *nori* to meet the needs of its population; however, due to increasing demand, as well as the continual pollution of coastal waters, much of Japan's *nori* is imported from Korea. *Nori* is commonly used as a wrap for *sushi* and *onigiri*, as well as a shredded or flaked topping for soups, rice and noodles.

Seafood

Seafood used in the preparation of *sushi* includes every imaginable species of marine life, including fish, shellfish, and their roe. The most common and popular varieties are tuna, yellowtail, salmon, shrimp, crab, squid, octopus, clams, eel, snapper, and mackerel. But this short list doesn't even begin to encompass the full range of *sushi* possibilities. Many varieties of seafood for *sushi* are seasonal, and although ocean-going marine life caught in its natural habitat is preferred, much of the seafood used for *sushi* is commercially raised.

Vegetables

In addition to the boundless variety of seafood ingredients used in the preparation of *sushi*, a number of vegetable ingredients are elemental as well. Fresh items such as green onion, *shiso* leaf, cucumber, avocado, and various types of seaweed add flavor, color and texture; while an array of pickled vegetables such as *daikon*, sour plums called *ume boshi*, fermented soybeans called *natto*, Chinese cabbage, carrots, bamboo, turnips, burdock root, ginger, Japanese cucumbers, and Japanese eggplant, add their own piquant flavor. 🍵

Wasabi

Wasabi

Condiments and Accompaniments

Shoyu

Shoyu is the Japanese word for soy sauce, one of the most important elements of Japanese cuisine. *Shoyu* is brewed from soybeans, water, salt and wheat, and there are many regional and proprietary variations. *Shoyu* is the basis for nearly every type of sauce or broth served with Japanese food, as well as a ubiquitous condiment. Some of the oldest companies in Japan are family-owned *shoyu* breweries.

Gari Shoga

Gari Shoga is the Japanese name for the pink pickled ginger commonly served as an accompaniment to *sushi*. *Gari shoga* is made from the large, knobby root of the ginger plant, *Zingiber officinale*. Sliced paper thin and marinated in sweetened rice wine vinegar, its peppery, perfumed flavor is the perfect palate cleanser between bites of *sushi*, and is also valued as a digestive agent.

Wasabi

The green paste commonly used as a seasoning agent and served as a condiment for *sushi* is called *wasabi*. Ground fresh from the root of an Asian plant known by the botanical name *Wasabia japonica*, or mixed into a paste from its powdered form, *wasabi* is quite peppery, although it doesn't linger on the lips like chili powder. It's more likely to give you a quick rush in your sinuses and disappear just as quickly. Some *sushi* lovers like to mix a little *wasabi* with the *shoyu*, which is perfectly fine if you like the taste. If not, it's okay to leave the *wasabi* untouched. Also, be aware that the *sushi* chef may dab a bit of *wasabi* inside each piece of *sushi*.

Daikon

Daikon is a large, carrot-shaped white radish (*Raphanus sativus*), commonly used in Japanese cuisine. A *daikon* can weigh up to seven pounds and is often served pickled, or finely shredded as an attractive garnish for some Japanese dishes, especially *sashimi*. Watching a sushi chef pare and julienne a *daikon* into a fine chiffonade by hand with his deathly sharp knife is truly a feat to behold.

Sunomono

A favorite way to begin a Japanese meal is with a light vinegared salad, and while you're waiting for your order to arrive, especially in upscale *sushi* bars, you might be served a tiny complimentary appetizer such as *sunomono* pickles, vinegared cucumber salad with bits of seafood, or *edamame*, soybeans in the pod.

Miso Shiru

Miso soup is a light, savory broth typically served before a Japanese meal. Traditional *miso* begins with a seaweed stóck called *dashi*, made from boiling *konbu* kelp and dried flakes of *katsuo* made from bonito, a type of large, flavorful ocean fish. The *konbu* and *katsuo* are filtered out, leaving a light, delicate broth, to which tiny flakes of dried *wakame* seaweed, small cubes of firm *tofu*, and a soybean paste called *miso* are added.

Miso is a fermented soybean paste widely used in traditional Japanese cuisine. There are two basic varieties of *miso*—white, and red—although the color of some other varieties of *miso* falls somewhere in between.

Miso is made by mixing steamed or boiled soybeans with salt and an *Aspergillus* fermenting agent called *koji*. Each region has its own unique style and flavor of *miso*. And although it is readily available at all Japanese markets, many Japanese housewives still make their own *miso*. *Miso* was first introduced to Japan from China in the eighth century, and its consumption was originally considered a luxury and was therefore limited to members of the ruling class and to Buddhist monks as a valuable protein supplement to their vegetarian diet. However, by the Muromachi Period (1392-1573), its popularity as a daily staple had spread to the common folk.

Commercial production of *miso* began in the 17th century, and each region developed its own unique *miso*, according to the available ingredients, the ecosystem, and the tastes of the local population. *Shiromiso* is favored in Kyoto, *hatchomiso* is the preferred style in Aichi Prefecture, and *shinshu miso*, the most widely consumed variety of *miso*, originated in Nagano Prefecture.

The average Japanese citizen consumes nearly 11 lbs. (5 kg.) of *miso* each year, and to keep up with the demand, approximately 1,400 Japanese *miso* companies produce more than a half million tons of *miso* annually. 🍚

Tsu

"Kampai!" - Beverages to Enjoy with *Sushi*

The traditional Japanese word associated with raising glasses in a toast is "*Kampai!*" It literally means 'empty the glass.' While any number of beverages for toasting and enjoying with your *sushi* experience may be offered on a contemporary *sushi* menu, from soft drinks to French Bordeaux and Napa Valley Chardonnay, the definitive beverage choices for the *sushi* purist are green tea, beer and *sake*, all of which may be enjoyed throughout the course of a single meal. These three beverages are the perfect complement for the delicate subtleties of the fish, the tang of the vinegar, the rush of the *wasabi*, the spice of the ginger, and the deep, salty bottom-note of the *shoyu*.

Without waiting for an order and free of charge, most *sushi* bars offer guests a steaming mug of green tea as soon as they arrive, and keep it filled throughout the meal. Thereafter, you may order beer or *sake* according to your individual taste. *Sake* is the beverage traditionally served with *sashimi*, while beer is appropriate to accompany everything else. But no one will frown if you prefer beer with your *sashimi*. Green tea should always be drunk plain, without adding cream or sugar.

Green Tea

Cha or *O-cha* is the Japanese word for green tea, which is served with nearly every Japanese meal. Green tea is derived from the same tea plant as the more commonly known black tea. However, the leaves used to make black tea are fermented before drying, but Japanese green tea is steamed to prevent fermentation, which results in the leaves retaining their green color. The steamed tea leaves are then rolled and dried.

Tea was introduced to Japan from China by Buddhist monks, who planted the first tea near Uji and Sakamoto in 805 A.D. At first, tea was used strictly for medicinal purposes, and then, only for the nobility. The Zen monk Eisai is attributed with popularizing it throughout the Buddhist monasteries as a means of staying awake during *zazen* meditation. Later, Shogun Ashikaga Yoshimasa encouraged the appreciation of tea by hosting ceremonial tastings, and thus the advent of the tea ceremony. However, tea remained the privilege of the aristocracy until Edo times (1603-1898) when its enjoyment spread to the wealthy merchant class and eventually to the common folk.

There are approximately 150,000 acres of tea cultivated in Japan to yield about 110,000 tons of tea leaves. There are many grades of Japanese green tea, from the garden variety leaves for everyday consumption, to the more refined and expensive powdered *matcha* used for the traditional Japanese tea ceremony. The most common varieties are: *Sencha Honyama*, a delicate green tea with a floral aroma; *Gyokuro*, a darker and more aromatic quality; and *Matcha*, the grassy and somewhat bitter tea powder used exclusively for the tea ceremony. *Bancha Houjicha* is a roasted tea with a nutty flavor and an amber color. *Bancha* is a low grade tea made from the stems and leaves left over from the primary harvest. *Genmaicha* is a blend of green tea, roasted rice and popcorn, popularized during the tea shortages of World War II.

The Japanese people enjoy other types of tea as well, including *kocha*, which is served European style with milk and sugar or with lemon, called *miruku tei* (milk tea) or *remon tei* (lemon tea). *Oolongcha* is Chinese oolong tea from Taiwan and China. *Mugicha* is brewed from barley and enjoyed cold during the hot and humid summer season. And *kombucha* is made from dried sea kelp.

Japanese Beer

Beer was first introduced to Japan by European trading companies in the 1850s. The Japanese people soon developed an appetite for the heady beverage, and since then, Japanese brewers have perfected the art. Beer has now surpassed *sake* as the leading alcoholic beverage consumed in Japan. The main producers of beer in Japan are Sapporo, Kirin, Asahi, and Suntory. Each different brand of Japanese beer has its own unique flavor and quality. Sapporo is a medium bodied beer, while Kirin is fuller bodied, and Asahi and Suntory tend to be crisp and dry. Japanese beer is available in both individual 12-ounce (355 ml.) bottles and in large, double-sized bottles perfect for sharing.

Sake

Sake, Japanese rice wine, also called *o-sake* or *nihon-shu*, is served in one of three ways: warmed, room temperature, or chilled. The most common presentation, called *atsukan sake*, is heated and served in a little ceramic carafe called *tokkuri*, accompanied by a tiny cup for sipping called a *choko* or *sakazuki*.

In the summer months, a cold-filtered variety called draft *sake* or *namazake* may also be served chilled. *Nama* means 'fresh,' and this variation is purified with microfilters instead of heat pasteurization, which preserves its essential flavors. *Namazake* is bottled immediately without aging, which produces a light, clean *sake* that should always be served chilled.

There is also an unfiltered variety of *sake* called *nigorizake*, which is milky white, slightly sweeter than the clear *sake*, and typically served during the summer months, although some *sushi* bars serve it year-round.

You might also see patrons at the *sushi* bar drinking *sake*, especially the unfiltered variety, out of little square wooden boxes called *masu*, a tradition that dates back to feudal times in Japan. Originally used as a measure for daily rations of rice, *masu* were sometimes used to measure portions of *sake* as well. It's a popular eccentricity in some establishments, where the boxes are filled to the brim and served on a saucer to catch the overflow. If you're served *sake* in a box, just be sure to sip it from the corner, otherwise it will dribble down your chin on both sides.

Types of *Sake*

With more than 3,000 *sake* breweries in Japan, quality, style, complexity, flavor, fragrance, and cost can all vary significantly from one label to the next, and *sake* classification is strictly established. Although there are numerous sub-categories, the two general classifications are *sake* made from rice and water only, and *sake* fortified with added alcohol.

In the classification made with only rice, there are three groups: *Junmai-Sake*, *Junmai-Ginjo*, and *Junmai-Dai-Ginjo*. In the classification with added alcohol, there are four groups, the lowest and largest of which is regular, generic *sake*, to which large amounts of alcohol is added. The other three categories are premium *sake*, called *Honjozo*, *Ginjo-Sake* and *Dai-Ginjo-Sake*, which only have a little alcohol added. The main difference between the grades in both groups is the degree to which the rice has been milled before brewing.

Ginjo-shu

Ginjo-shu is the Japanese term for premium or reserve quality *sake*, the very best. Production of *ginjo* grade *sake* requires the very best rice, the purest water, a special type of yeast for slow fermentation, and a longer brewing process. The result is a markedly superior *sake*, refined in texture, and rich, fruity and floral in both taste and aroma. Predictably, *ginjo-shu* is costly, elegantly packaged, and served only in the finest establishments.

Fatsu-shu

Fatsu-shu is the Japanese classification for regular, everyday *sake*. Somewhat sweeter and lighter-bodied than *ginjo grade sake*, *fatsu-shu* is served as the 'house brand' in many *sushi* bars, and is commonly available at supermarkets and liquor stores.

Most sake sold and served in the U.S. is called *kara-kuchi*, a 'dry' style; however, there is another slightly sweeter variety called *ama-kuchi. Sake* is typically available in large bottles called *isho-bin*, but is also available in smaller 25 oz. (750 ml.) bottles as well.

To avail themselves of lower overhead costs and the abundance of less expensive California rice, several of the larger Japanese *sake* breweries, including Gekkeikan, Ozeki, and Takara have established facilities in the U.S.

The History of *Sake*

The history of *sake* dates back to the Nara Period (710-94 B.C.), shortly after rice cultivation was introduced from China during the third century B.C. Sake was first produced at the imperial court and in Shinto shrines, where it was used in religious ceremonies. The first *sake* produced in Japan was called *kuchikami no sake*, which literally means 'chewing in the mouth,' a name derived from the primitive religious ritual of partially chewing the rice and regurgitating it into a fermentation vat. The chewing process provided the enzymes necessary for fermentation, until it was discovered that yeast and *koji*, a mold enzyme, could be substituted as an agent to start the fermentation process.

During the early feudal era, each clan or village produced its own *sake* from locally-grown rice. However, over time, rice became a major agricultural industry in Japan, and with it, the mass production of *sake* developed as a commercial industry. Although it still played an important role in the Shinto religion, by the 14th century, *sake* was the most popular and widely consumed beverage in Japan, especially among the aristocracy. The fining process was discovered in the 1600s when a saboteur attempted to ruin a batch of *sake* by adding ashes to it, which rendered the sake crystal clear instead. The Industrial Revolution that took place after the Meiji Restoration in 1868 brought about further improvements in the *sake*-brewing process, including commercial presses, filtration devices and bottling facilities.

Although the technology of rice wine production is vastly different from its humble beginnings as '*kuchikami no sake*,' its noble place in Japanese culture and tradition has remained unchanged for centuries.

Other Japanese Beverages
Ume-shu

Ume-shu is a strong, sweet Japanese plum wine, served either warm or chilled. Light, fruity, and pale pink, *ume-shu* is sometimes poured over fruit for a fresh dessert. *Ume-shu* is favored for its tonic and digestive benefits, and many people make their own plum wine at home during the summer season by soaking sour plums and sugar in a clear alcoholic spirit called *shochu*.

Budo-shu

Budo-shu is the Japanese word for wine made from grapes. Japan has its own wine region in Yamanshi Prefecture in the foothills of Mt. Fuji, where they grow grapes in the traditional French style, including classic varietals such as cabernet sauvignon, sauvignon blanc and Johannesburg Riesling. Grape cultivation is a highly refined art in Japan, where each individual cluster of grapes is sheltered by its own little paper cone to protect it from the elements.

The first commercial Japanese winery was established in 1875 in Katsunuma, which is now a part of Mercian winery, the second largest company in Japan. Suntory also produces a line of varietal wines. However, not all wines produced in Japan are made from domestic grapes. The crop produced by the Yamanashi growing region is quite limited, and Japanese winemakers must rely on imported grapes and juice from Europe and the U.S. to meet the demand.

Sho-chu

Sho-chu is the Japanese name for a distilled spirit made with malted rice for fermentation, derived from the lees of *sake* production. *Shochu* is stronger than *sake* and has always been favored by the working class. There are two types of *shochu*. The standard type, *Otsu*, is made with raw sugar and is distilled in pot stills, while the *Ko* type is made with molasses. The alcohol content of *shochu* varies from 40 to 90 proof (20 to 45 percent), and averages 50 proof. *Shochu* may be drunk plain, or may be mixed with other ingredients for cocktails. 🍶

What's What at a *Sushi* Bar

The People
Chorishi – A licensed chef.

Itamae – A Japanese chef.

Shokunin – A master *sushi* chef.

Tools of the Trade
Baran – Sheets of bright green plastic, cut into intricate decorative shapes for *sushi* garnish.

Choriki – A mandolin-style vegetable shredder.

Daidokoro – The kitchen.

Hachi-maki – The headband worn by a *sushi* chef

Hangiri – A lidless wooden tub used to hold *sushi* rice as it cools. Its wide, shallow design facilitates the cooling process by providing a wide surface area for fanning the rice.

Happi – A short, wrapped tunic worn by *sushi* chefs.

Hocho – The Japanese word for culinary knives.

Hone-nuki – Boning tweezers.

Katsunobushi bako – A device for shaving dried bonito fish into fine flakes.

Kine – A pestle for grinding herbs and spices.

Kome-agezaru – A shallow, round-bottomed stainless steel and wire mesh basket used as a colander.

Kushi – A bamboo skewer.

Kyusu – A teapot.

Makisu – A small split-bamboo mat used to make snug, uniform rolls of *makizushi*.

Manaita – A cutting board used by the *sushi* chef.

Mori Hashi – Special chopsticks used for arranging *sashimi*.

Mushiki – A metal or bamboo steamer.

Niki-ita – A rectangular board with runners on the bottom for serving *sushi* or for stacking to store prepared foods, such as dried fish.

Ohachi – A wooden tub with a flat lid, used for storing *sushi* rice at the chef's *sushi* preparation area. Also called *ohitsu*.

Ohitsu – A wooden tub with a flat lid, used for storing *sushi* rice at the chef's *sushi* preparation area. Also called *ohachi*.

Oroshi-gane – A sharp-toothed vegetable grater, used for turning fresh ingredients such as *daikon* radish, ginger, and *wasabi* into a fine pulp.

Oshiki – A serving tray for *tatami* dining.

Oshiwaku – A wooden box with a lid, used for making pressed *sushi*, Osaka-style.

Otama – A soup ladle. Also called *otama-jakushi*.

Otama-jakushi – A soup ladle. Also called *otama*.

Sai-bashi – Extra long chopsticks, used in the kitchen for handling food during cooking.

Sarashi – A cotton terrycloth kitchen towel.

Sasara – A bamboo scouring brush.

Saya – A wooden sheath for protecting the blade of a *sushi* knife.

Seiri – A steamer box.

Shamoji – A small paddle used to mix and serve rice, usually made of wood, but modern versions may be made of plastic.

Shichiren – A small, portable clay brazier that burns charcoal for grilling meat or fish.

Suribachi – A mortar-like ceramic bowl with a rough inner surface, used with a wooden pestle to grind or pulverize various spices and fresh ingredients.

Surikogi – A wooden pestle used with a *suribachi* bowl for grinding and pulverizing spices and fresh ingredients.

Tamago-yaki – A rectangular omelet pan used for making the egg omelet called *tamago*.

Tare-haki – A brush used for applying sauces to certain types of *sushi*.

Tare-ire – A container used to hold sauce.

Tawashi – A straw vegetable scrubber.

To-ishi – A whetstone used for sharpening knives.

Uchiwa – A flat, paper fan with bamboo ribs and handle, used for fanning *sushi* rice to accelerate the cooling process.

Uroko otoshi – A hand-held device for removing fish scales.

Zaru – A shallow, round-bottomed basket used as a colander. The modern stainless steel and wire mesh version is called *kome-agezaru*.

About the Knives

Japanese culinary knives are called *hocho*, and each *sushi* chef has his own set. Forged from carbon steel, a chef's knives are the most important tools of his craft, with a tradition that dates back to feudal times and the forging of the *samurai* sword. The process used to forge the most magnificent and legendary *samurai* blades is the same technique still used to craft the finest *sushi* knives today. The forging and tempering process yields a *hocho* blade that is strong, durable, and precise, with an ability to hold a keen edge.

There are two basic methods of blade production: *Honyaki* and *Kasumi*. The *Honyaki*-style forging process, called *hizukuri*, begins as a rod of solid, high-carbon steel, which is heated red-hot, and hammered to purify the steel and form the basic shape of the knife. Next, the steel is tempered in a process called *yaki-ire*, using either water to yield a hard, brittle blade, or oil to yield a more durable, flexible blade. The result is a solid steel knife that holds its edge, but requires extra effort to maintain.

The second basic forging process is called *kasumi-bocho*, in which layers of malleable iron are forged over a high-carbon steel core. The resulting blade is softer and therefore dulls more quickly but takes less time to sharpen.

The hand-forging process takes several skilled craftsmen, some of whom are descended from *samurai* swordsmiths, two weeks to create, and a single *sushi* knife can range in price from about $50 for a basic *tatsutogi* grade knife, to more than $3,000 for the finest *honyaki* grade blade. However, some cutlery companies are now using industrial automation to reduce the labor-intensive cost of forging *sushi* knives.

Once the forging process is complete, the edge of a sushi knife is honed to a bevel on only the right side of the blade. This style is called *kataba*, and its shape facilitates ease of use to prevent dragging and to produce perfect filets and slices.

Each *sushi* ingredient and slicing technique requires a specific type of *sushi* knife, and Japanese knives are classified according to their shape and purpose.

There are two types of *sashimi* knives: *yanagiba* and *takobiki*. The *yanagiba* style was developed in the Kansai region near Osaka. Its name means 'willow-shaped,' to describe its deep, pointed blade. *Takobiki* means 'octopus knife,' and this style of *sushi* blade, used mainly in the Kanto area surrounding Tokyo, is thin and blunt-tipped. Both styles range from 8 to 13 in. (20 to 33 cm.) in length, and 3⁄4 to 1 1⁄4 in. (2 to 3 cm.) in depth.

Another type of *sushi* knife is the *deba*, used for rugged tasks such as cleaning fish, and cutting through bones, tough meat or cartilage, and thick vegetable rinds. Their blades are heavy and sturdy, ranging from 4 to 8 in. (10 to 20 cm.) long, and up to 2 1⁄2 in. (6 cm.) deep, with both the upper and lower edges tapering to a sharp tip.

A smaller knife, called the *kodeba* is used for intricate tasks such as cleaning small fish and shellfish.

The *usuba* is yet another type of knife especially designed for peeling, slicing, and chopping vegetables. It has a straight-edged blade, much like a fine meat cleaver and may be sharpened on one or both sides.

The *sushi* chef also uses other specialized types of knives for opening shellfish, preparing eel, and sculpting vegetables.

Because they are not typically made of stainless steel, *sushi* knives will rust if not properly maintained and stored. They must be washed, dried, oiled, and hand-sharpened each day, using whetstones specifically textured and graded for each type of blade. *Sushi* knives are then slipped into wooden sheaths called *saya*, and wrapped in a soft, protective case.

Tableware
Bento – A special compartmented serving container for boxed lunches. Although they are typically used for carrying food on the go, some restaurants also serve certain meals *bento*-style.

Cha-wan – A green tea mug. Also called *yunomi.*

Cha-budai – A dobin teapot.

Chiri renge – A Chinese soup spoon.

Geta – A small wooden board with rectangular risers on the bottom, used by some *sushi* bars for serving pickled ginger and *wasabi,* and as a surface on which to place individual orders of *sushi.* The same word is used for the traditional raised wooden sandals with cloth thongs, also called *geta.*

Hashi – The Japanese word for chopsticks, also called *o-hashi.* However, most *sushi* bars use the disposable variety of chopsticks, known as *wari-bashi.* This term is a combination of 'wari,' which means 'divide,' and the euphonic pronunciation of *hashi,* which becomes '*bashi*' when combined with a prefix.

Choko – Tiny cups for sipping *sake.*

Hashi oki – A small ceramic piece for resting chopsticks when not in use.

Masu – Small wooden boxes used for serving unfiltered *sake,* a tradition that dates back to feudal times in Japan. Originally used as a measure for daily rations of rice, *masu* were sometimes used to measure portions of *sake* as well. It's a popular eccentricity in some establishments, where the boxes are filled to the brim and served on a saucer to catch the overflow. Some *sushi* bars even write the names of their regular patrons on the *masu* and keep them behind the bar for use each time they visit.

Oshibori – Before enjoying a meal at a Japanese restaurant, especially *sushi,* patrons are offered *oshibori,* small, damp terrycloth towels for cleansing the hands. In winter months, the towels are served steaming hot, while in the hot, humid summer months, they are served refreshingly chilled. *Oshibori* should be used for cleansing the hands only, never for wiping the face or for mopping up spills throughout the meal.

Renge – A Chinese soup spoon.

Sakazuki – Tiny cups for sipping warm *sake*. Also called *choko*.

Sara – A general term for dishes and plates.

Sushi-oke – Decorative dishes for serving *sushi*, available in an endless variety of shapes, sizes and decorative motifs to enhance the presentation of the chef's edible art.

Tokkuri – A small ceramic carafe for serving warm *sake*. They come in many shapes with decorative Japanese motifs; however, many *sushi* bars use *tokkuri* imprinted with their logos.

Wari-bashi – Disposable wooden chopsticks. See 'hashi.'

Yunomi – A straight-sided, handle-less ceramic mug for serving Japanese green tea. Each *sushi* bar has its own decorative design, some imprinted with their logos, others decorated with stylized Japanese motifs, or reproductions of *ukiyo-e* woodblock prints. One classic *yunomi* design features dozens of *kanji* characters for the various types of fish, written vertically down the sides of the cup, with the pronunciations written in tiny *furigana* characters next to them.

Zataku – A low table for dining on *tatami* mats.

Furnishings
Chochin
The Japanese name for a paper lantern, made of rice paper glued to a square or circular bamboo frame. *Chochin* were first used in Japan in the 17th century, and are classified according to the style of the region in which they were made. Even with the advent of electricity, *chochin* are still a common fixture in modern Japan, and can be seen in restaurants and homes, or as decorations during festival times.

Noren
Noren are traditional curtains hung in entryways and other doorways in both homes and businesses. *Noren* come in several lengths and are split into two or more panels. They often bear family crests, auspicious symbols, company logos, or the name of what's available inside the shop. *Noren* are most often dyed indigo blue with white markings, although they do come in other colors. The use of *noren* dates back to the Heian Period (784-1185 A.D.) when they were thought to ward off evil spirits, and later in the Muromachi Period in shops and restaurants as convenient buffers for dust and harsh sunlight through which customers could easily come and go. Today, *noren* are still a common sight in homes and businesses throughout Japan.

Ryori-sanpuru
Ryori-sanpuru is the Japanese name for the artificial food displays in the windows of most restaurants in Japan. The word is literally derived from *ryori*, the Japanese word for cooking, and the 'Japanized' version of the English word 'sample.' These colorful and remarkably realistic representations of the restaurant's menu selection are an effective enticement to lure passers-by inside for a meal. The *ryori-sanpuru* business in Japan is a multi-billion yen industry.

Tsuke-dai
The wooden counter around which patrons sit and on which *sushi* is served.

Tatami
Tatami is the Japanese name for the woven straw mats used for flooring since the 17th century in traditional Japanese homes, tea houses, temples, shrines, restaurants, and various other types of buildings. *Tatami* mats are composed of a 2 in. (5 cm.) thick compressed, rice straw core, covered with a fragrant, finely woven grass, and bound at the edges with a border of decorative brocade ribbon. *Tatami* mats were originally woven by hand, but for today's modern homes and businesses, commercially produced *tatami* mats are now available. Freshly woven *tatami* are springy and pale green, but eventually they dry and yellow over time. Therefore, the tradition is to replace *tatami* mats as frequently as possible, ideally every spring.

Although the size of *tatami* varies from one region to the next, they are always twice as long as they are wide, approximately 1 m. by 2 m. (3.3 ft. by 6.6 ft.). When two *tatami* are placed side by side, they form a perfect square called a *tsubo*, which are placed perpendicular to each other in an alternating pattern. Japanese rooms are measured by the number of *tatami* mats they contain, with most rooms in typical homes and apartments being four, six or eight mats. However, some of the larger shrines, temples, and pavilions appear to have acres of *tatami* to accommodate the resident priests and monks in their daily chanting, and the crowds of worshippers who come to visit on special occasions.

To accommodate irregularly proportioned rooms, *tatami* may be divided into half mats called *hanjo*. Tea houses also feature *tatami* floors, but because some of them are so tiny, special three-quarter mats called *daimedatami* may be necessary. *Tatami* floors are the perfect surface for meditation, eating at low tables, and sleeping on futons. However, they are fragile and therefore, in the interest of keeping them as clean and undamaged as possible, shoes are never worn in a *tatami* room.

Decorative Figures

Daruma Dolls

Daruma dolls are traditional symbols of determination and accomplishment. An interesting legend and significance is associated with these ubiquitous bright red dolls. The spherical papier mâché figures are hand-painted in red and gold, and represent a Buddhist monk who, according to legend, sat in meditation for seven years, until his arms and legs atrophied. It is even said that he cut off his own eyelids so that he could stay awake during meditation, which is why *Daruma* dolls have no arms, legs or eyes. Today, *Daruma* dolls are a symbol of resolution and dedication to a task. When a person is committed to an important goal, the left eye of the doll is painted in, and once the goal is accomplished, the right eye is added to symbolize success.

Fukusuke

A figure of a kneeling man bowing deeply, placed at the entrance of *sushi* restaurants to signify respect, appreciation and gratitude. The *fukusuke* symbolizes bowing to customers as a sign of welcome when they arrive, and bowing to customers when they leave as a way of saying thank you.

Maneki-neko

A statue of a white, waving cat, often displayed as a symbol of good luck and prosperity. An amusing bit of Japanese folklore is associated with the *maniki neko*, whose image can be seen beckoning from shop windows all over Japan. As the story goes, on the outskirts of old Tokyo, which was called Edo in ancient times, in a place called *Setagaya*, there was a small temple called *Gotokuji*, where there lived a beautiful white cat. The monks of the temple loved the white cat. Each day, the cat would sit on the veranda of the temple and watch all the travelers on the road to Edo.

Sometimes, a weary traveler would stop by the temple to rest in the shady garden and pray for a safe journey. Whenever someone stopped by, the white cat always got a scratch under its chin, or behind its ears, and a few strokes of its silky white fur.

One stormy day, however, there were no visitors to the temple, and the monks stayed inside all day to keep out of the cold, wet weather. Just before dark, the white cat was curled up in his favorite spot on the veranda when he heard the sound of horse's hooves on the road, and soon there appeared a great *daimyo* warrior named Lord Ii on horseback. Seeing the temple, he stopped in hopes of finding a warm, dry place to get out of the rain. But the temple was dark and the doors and shutters were all fastened tight, so the *daimyo* didn't see much point in getting off his horse to knock at the temple door.

Just then, the white cat sat upright and raised its paw at the *daimyo*, almost as if to wave hello. Feeling certain that the cat was waving at him, the *daimyo* was astonished at the gesture, and got down off his horse to get a closer look. As he passed through the temple gate and approached the waving cat, he heard a crackle overhead and turned just in time to see a blinding thunderbolt strike the ground where he had stood only moments earlier.

The *daimyo* leapt to safety on the veranda, and the monks inside the temple came out to see what was causing the noise and commotion. The *daimyo* told them his miraculous tale of how the white cat had waved at him and saved his life. The monks gave the *daimyo* a hot meal and lodgings for the night, and from that day on, the *daimyo* sent money to the temple every month to pay for its upkeep and to care for the white cat that had saved his life.

Today, statues and figurines of waving white cats called *maneki-neko* are considered good luck, and can be seen at the entrances of many restaurants and shops throughout Japan.

Tanuki

Tanuki is the Japanese word for a badger, a creature indigenous to Japan and an important figure in Japanese folklore. *Tanuki* are believed to have supernatural powers, including the ability to transform themselves into humans, especially monks and beautiful women. In Japanese folk tales, they are fond of drinking *sake*, and they make drumming sounds on their round bellies during the full moon. Images of smiling *tanuki* with rotund bellies, standing on their hind legs, are often placed at the entrances of entertainment establishments such as bars and pleasure houses. *Tanuki* may also be used as a nickname for a crafty individual, and the term *tanukineiri* means to feign sleeping, akin to the term 'playing possum.' A dish called *tanukisoba* is made with buckwheat noodles in a savory broth topped with *tempura* fritters. A similar version called *tanukiudon* may be made with thick white *udon* noodles.

A Trick for the Tanuki (A Tale from Japanese Folklore)

Once upon a time, in the hillsides overlooking Kyoto, there was a tiny shrine, dedicated to the *kami* spirit of the mountain. The old priest who tended the shrine was very fond of *tempura*, and he often made it for his supper. Whenever the temple patrons brought him gifts of fish or fresh vegetables, the old priest would cook up a tasty batch of *tempura*, and of course, he always saved the best piece to place on the altar as an offering to the *kami* spirit of the mountain.

In the hillside overlooking the shrine, there also lived a *tanuki*, a fat, mischievous old badger who liked to play tricks on the priest. Sometimes he would knock at the temple gate, and when the priest came to answer, the *tanuki* would disappear into the hedge to laugh as the priest scratched his head and wondered if he was hearing things again. And sometimes the *tanuki* would hide the old priest's sandals, leaving two pine-cones on the doorstep in their place. He would sneak into the shrine and turn the prayer scrolls upside down, he would pick peonies from the garden before the blossoms had opened, and he would leave a trail of acorns around the veranda for the priest to sweep away every day.

But the *tanuki's* favorite trick to play on the old priest was to steal the gifts of food he left on the altar of the shrine for the *kami* spirit of the mountain. The *tanuki* liked every kind of food except *tempura*, the old priest's favorite dish. It's not that he didn't like the tasty fish and fresh vegetables inside, it was the crunchy batter on the outside that he didn't love. So whenever the priest made *tempura* for his supper and left the best piece on the altar for the *kami* spirit of the mountain, the mischievous *tanuki* would sneak into the temple at night and steal only the fish or vegetables inside, leaving the empty *tempura* batter behind.

For many months, the old priest thought perhaps the *kami* spirit did not like *tempura*; nevertheless, he left an offering on the altar each time he made it for his supper. But one night, the old priest heard a noise outside his window near the shrine. By the light of the full moon, he saw the fat shadow of the crafty badger creep into the shrine, and slip out again with something in its paws. The priest went out to the shrine, where he found that the tasty bit of fish that had been cooked inside the crunchy *tempura* was gone, and only the batter had been left behind. "Ah ha!" he thought to himself. "So it is the *tanuki*, and not the *kami*, who doesn't like *tempura*."

This gave him an idea. Since it was the crunchy *tempura* that the old priest loved best, no matter what fish or vegetable was inside it, he began frying the *tempura* batter up all by itself with no filling at all, and eating it with tasty *soba* noodles, a dish he liked to call *tanuki soba*. And whenever he made it, he would leave an offering of empty *tempura* batter on the altar of the shrine, knowing that the crafty old badger wouldn't touch it, and the *kami* spirit of the mountain would always be sure to receive his gift. ✾

Tsu

Wasabi

A Typical Visit to a *Sushi* Bar

Irashai Mase!

When you walk through the door of any *sushi* bar, you'll likely be met with a chorus of "*Irashai Mase!*" A greeting that essentially means, "Come on in!" In most places, you will be seated by a hostess, and if you haven't already made reservations, you'll enjoy the best experience if you request a seat at the *sushi* bar, which, if it's full when you arrive, is well worth the wait for a vacant chair. At the *sushi* bar, you get a front row seat from which to watch the *sushi* chef practice his craft.

Speed of services varies from place to place, but the first rule of thumb in a *sushi* bar is to relax and be patient. It's all about the trip, and not the destination, remember? Japanese cuisine is a highly evolved culinary art, and these things take time.

Chances are, the first thing you'll be served is an *oshibori*, a steaming terry washcloth for cleansing your hands. It will probably be served in a bamboo basket or a dish of some type. It will be slightly damp and might be quite hot, so use it with caution. When you're done with it, fold it neatly and place it back in its original serving dish. And remember, it's only intended for cleansing your hands, so please don't wipe your face with it, and don't use it throughout the meal to mop up anything you've dropped or spilled.

The next thing to arrive will probably be a mug of *agiri* or *ocha*, Japanese green tea. It's complimentary and quite delicious. This light brew has an ever-so-slightly bitter taste that goes perfectly with the flavors of the meal that awaits you. But as warm and soothing as it is, be aware that green tea is loaded with caffeine, so imbibe accordingly.

If you're in the mood for something a little more potent, beer or *sake* will also be available. The beer choices are likely to include Sapporo, Kirin, Asahi and possibly Suntory. Each has its own unique flavor and quality. Sapporo is a medium bodied beer, while Kirin is fuller bodied, and Asahi and Suntory tend to be crisp and dry.

Sake, Japanese rice wine, is served in one of three ways. The most common presentation is heated and served in a little ceramic carafe accompanied by a tiny cup for sipping. However, in the summer months, *sake* may also be served chilled, and there is an unfiltered variety, which is milky white and slightly sweeter than the clear *sake*. You might also see patrons at the *sushi* bar drinking *sake* out of little square wooden boxes. It's a popular eccentricity in some establishments; if you're served *sake* in a box, just be sure to sip it from the corner, otherwise it will dribble down your chin on both sides.

What to Order

By now, it's probably time to order. The waitress tending patrons at the bar will take your beverage order from over your shoulder. However, in some cases, she may take your food order as well. Otherwise, you will have to order directly from *itamae-san*, the *sushi* chef. If you order food from the waitress, you may want to request all your dishes at once. But if you order from the chef, you may wish to order one or two dishes at a time, gradually working your way up to increasingly more exotic fare as the evening progresses. However, the one-dish-at-a-time method usually takes a little longer, as the chef is serving everyone in the restaurant simultaneously. Don't be shy, but don't be impatient either. Wait for an opportunity to catch his eye and tell him quickly and clearly what you would like to order. He'll add it to the running list of orders in his head and will prepare it for you when your turn comes. And remember, only order beverages from the waitress, not from the chef.

Many *sushi* bars have a combination plate that features a variety of items, and often includes a bowl of *miso* soup. This is an excellent way to sample several things at once. However, in addition to the more common varieties of fish, combination plates are also likely to include a couple of exotic items such as roe, eel or octopus. If you're not quite ready to take this daring leap, you may wish to request a substitute for those items.

But if you're feeling more adventurous, the possibilities are endless, as *sushi* comes in many forms. *Nigiri sushi*, also called *nigirizushi*, is the most basic and common. It comes in pairs, and usually consists of an oblong ball of vinegared rice topped with a single perfect slice of raw fish. Simple and delicious. Some of the more palatable and popular toppings for *nigiri sushi* include:

Tuna – Japanese name: *maguro*. A rosy-pink, fine textured, mildly flavored ocean fish.

Yellowtail – Japanese name: *hamachi*. A creamy, firm-fleshed, mildly flavored ocean fish.

Salmon – Japanese name: *sake*. A slightly-salty, orange ocean fish.

Halibut – Japanese name: *hirame*. A mild flavored, firm white ocean fish.

Snapper – Japanese name: *tai*. A delicately flavored translucent ocean fish.

Mackerel – Japanese name: *saba*. A strongly flavorful, ocean-going fish.

Shrimp – Japanese name: *ebi*. Usually served cooked, but certain types are also available raw in some places.

Scallop – Japanese name: *hotategai*. A creamy, fine textured shellfish.

Egg Omelet – Japanese name: *tamago*. A slice of chilled egg omelet.

In addition to the basic *nigiri* pairs, the term *sushi* also includes a rolled variety called *sushi maki* or *makizushi*, which contains the same basic elements as *nigiri sushi*, with the added feature of a crisp, dark green, paper-thin seaweed wrapper called *nori*. The *sushi* chef spreads a layer of vinegared rice on the *nori*, topped with a seafood filling, then firmly wraps the whole thing, cigar-style, and then slices it into six bite-sized pieces. Although anything may be tucked inside a roll of *makizushi*, the most common and popular variations include:

Tuna roll – Japanese name: *tekka maki*. Seaweed paper wrapped around rice and raw tuna.

Cucumber roll – Japanese name: *kappa maki*. Seaweed paper wrapped around rice and strips of fresh cucumber.

California roll – A seaweed paper wrapper filled with rice, imitation crab legs and avocado, and sometimes sprinkled with sesame seeds.

As an alternative to the simple cigar-style rolls, when the cut rolls are stood on end, with the rice filling inside pressed toward the bottom, it leaves a perfect little niche for filling with scoops of fish roe or other minced and spiced seafood. This style of *sushi* is called *gunkan-maki*. And then there's *futomaki*, an oversized *makizushi* roll filled with a colorful assortment of cucumber, red ginger, pink fish cake, dried gourd, pickled yellow radish, and egg omelet.

Another variation of *makizushi* is *temaki*, the hand roll, in which a sheet of *nori* is loosely filled with various ingredients and rolled into a large cone. Of course, by definition, a hand roll must be hand-held and consumed in multiple bites.

Although technically not categorized as *sushi*, a simply elegant item you may find on the *sushi* bar menu is *sashimi*, several perfect slices of raw fish served with nothing more than a simple garnish of shredded *daikon* radish. *Sashimi* is also served *chirashi*-style, with assorted vegetables atop vinegared *sushi* rice. *Sashimi* should be ordered as a first course, and the traditional beverage to accompany it is *sake*.

And Now for Something Completely Different...

If you're feeling adventuresome, there's a whole new world of flavors and textures awaiting you at your local *sushi* bar. Those with an open mind and an intrepid palate might want to try:

Eel

Japanese name: *unagi* or *anago*. There are two varieties of this snake-like creature, freshwater or ocean-going, both of which are usually served broiled with a sweet soy glaze called *tsume*. It has a surprisingly mild flavor and a fine texture. Slices of *unagi* or *anago* may be prepared either as *nigiri* or *makizushi*.

Raw Shrimp

Japanese name: *ama ebi*. Translucent pairs of sweet, cold-water shrimp are served raw, and a few minutes later, their crispy-fried heads are served up with eyes, whiskers, and tentacles intact. Sounds awful...tastes great! Crunch, crunch. Yum, yum.

Flying Fish Roe

Japanese name: *tobiko*. These tiny, bright orange fish eggs are usually served in generous scoops inside the hollowed out niches of *gunkan-maki* rolls. They are mildly fishy and salty, and when you bite down on them, each tiny egg explodes with a delicate pop. You will also find *tobiko* used in small amounts, sprinkled as a colorful garnish on other *sushi* items. And if you're feeling especially daring, order the *tobiko* topped with a raw quail egg, *uzura no tamago*.

Salmon Roe

Japanese name: *ikura*. These luscious fish eggs look like bright orange capsules that ooze their salty juices when you bite down on them. Typically served as *gunkan-maki*.

Squid

Japanese name: *ika*. Also known as cuttlefish, the flesh of this pearlescent sea creature tends to be a little chewy, and therefore is best consumed in a single, long-lasting bite.

Octopus

Japanese name: *tako*. One of the most beautiful items in the *sushi* chef's display case, the opaque white flesh of the octopus, tinged with the rosy purple of its suction cups, is cut into cross sections and served *nigiri* style, or diced and spiced for a *gunkan-maki* topping. But be advised that *tako* is among the most rubbery of all *sushi*.

Sea Urchin

Japanese name: *uni*. Inside the delicate purple and white globe of its translucent shell hides the mustard-colored blob that is the sea urchin, technically its reproductive organs. The taste of this somewhat pricey, unique sea creature, which is only in season from August through April, was once described by a *sushi*-loving friend of mine as "the flavors of an entire tidepool distilled into a single bite." I couldn't have said it better myself. You'll either love it...or you'll hate it, but you gotta try it at least once.

Horseneck Clam
Japanese name: *mirugai*. Also known as the geoduck, this oceanic oddity resembles a certain part of the male anatomy, which shall remain nameless. You'll know it when you see it. Order it if you dare.

The Chef's Special
Nearly every *sushi* bar offers a tempting array of creative variations on the basic *sushi* bar fare. They're often the result of the chef's culinary visions, and although they tend to be a bit more pricey than *nigiri* and *makizushi*, they can be quite tasty and creative. You'll usually find them written on a chalkboard displayed on the wall behind the *sushi* chef, with colorful names like "*Rock & Roll*," "*Tsunami Tuna*," and "*Year of the Dragon*."

Condiments and Side Dishes
Sushi is always accompanied by several additional items to complement and enhance the flavor of the fish itself. *Shoyu* (what we Westerners call soy sauce) is usually provided at the *sushi* bar. It may come in the original, individually labeled bottle, or more likely, in a little ceramic pot with a spout. Your place at the *sushi* bar will also be set with a shallow dish to hold the *shoyu* for dipping. But be careful when pouring the *shoyu* into the dish, as it comes splashing out and is very easy to spill. If there's a little hole in the lid of the container,

place your finger over it to help control the flow of the *shoyu*. While you're waiting for your order to arrive, especially in upscale *sushi* bars, you might be served a tiny complimentary appetizer such as vinegared cucumber salad, or *edamame*, soybeans in the pod. Just before your *sushi* arrives, if you're lucky and have ordered wisely, you'll be served a steaming bowl of *miso* soup. For those of you who have never had the pleasure, this is one of the most comforting foods you will ever consume. *Miso* soup is composed of a savory broth steeped with *kazuo*, flakes of smoked bonito, and *kombu*, dried sea kelp. To that, a generous dollop of *miso*, a soybean paste much like peanut butter, is added, along with tiny cubes of *tofu* and perhaps bits of spring onion, or a delicate seaweed called *wakame*. As the *miso* dissolves, the whole bowl melts into a creamy infusion that is one of the kindest, most satisfying foods you will ever put in your tummy. *Miso* soup is not typically served with a spoon, so don't be shy. It's perfectly acceptable to pick up the bowl and sip directly from it, using your chopsticks to eat the *tofu* and seaweed.

When your *sushi* finally arrives, it will be accompanied by another small dish or two containing a mound of *gari shoga*, thinly shaved pickled ginger, and a little green ball of *wasabi*, a type of powdered Japanese radish mixed with water to form a paste. The *gari shoga* is quite tasty, and you may be tempted to eat it all by itself. But remember, it's not a salad, it's there as a palate cleanser to enhance the flavor of the *sushi*. The *wasabi* paste is quite peppery, although it doesn't linger on the lips like chili powder. It's more likely to give you a quick rush in your sinuses and disappear just as quickly. Some *sushi* lovers like to mix a little *wasabi* with the *shoyu*, which is perfectly fine if you like the taste. If not, it's okay to leave the *wasabi* untouched. Also, be aware that the *sushi* chef may dab a bit of *wasabi* inside each piece of *sushi*.

Faking It – For the Neophyte and the Faint of Heart

If, after reading all these descriptions of the pleasures that await you on your first visit to a *sushi* bar, you still can't get past the idea of consuming raw fish, there are a number of tasty cooked or non-fish items on the typical *sushi* menu. Your best bets are:

Ebi – Cooked shrimp served *nigiri* style on oblong balls of vinegared rice.

Kappa Maki – Fresh cucumber with vinegared rice wrapped in seaweed paper.

Tamago – A slice of chilled egg omelet served *nigiri* style on oblong balls of vinegared rice.

California roll – A seaweed paper wrapper with the rice rolled on the outside, and filled with imitation crab legs, cucumber and avocado, sprinkled with sesame seeds.

If any of these items appeal to you, feel free to order multiple portions of each. There's no rule that says you have to only order one of any given item.

Another Reassuring Thought

In addition to *sushi*, many Japanese restaurants offer other traditional dishes such as *Teriyaki* Chicken, battered and deep-fried *tempura*, and a wide variety of tasty noodle dishes. But be a sport. Go ahead and try a little *sushi* anyway.

A Little Local Color

Each *sushi* bar has its own ambiance. And while some are quite serene and sedate, you may find the atmosphere at your local *sushi* bar much more convivial. The intimacy of the chairs arranged around the preparation area is conducive to conversation, and each *sushi* chef tends to develop his own regular clientele. Temperament and disposition varies from one *sushi* chef to another, running the gamut from the strictly-business type who keeps his head down and focuses exclusively on his craft, to the chatty capers and showmanship of a world-class entertainer. If the one who presides over your first *sushi* experience is of the latter variety, by all means, feel free to strike up a conversation and get acquainted.

Other *Sushi* Venues

While a front row seat at the *sushi* bar is the most entertaining way to enjoy your first *sushi* experience, there are a couple of other *sushi* settings that you may find to your liking as well.

The Tatami Room

Many *sushi* bars also have small, secluded rooms with woven rice straw *tatami* floors, small cushions or legless chairs and low tables for enjoying your meal in intimate privacy. This is a uniquely pleasant setting for small groups and special occasions, but usually has to be reserved in advance.

Sushi-Go-Round

There's an alternative to the traditional *sushi* bar that is growing in popularity. Actually it's an adaptation of a type of Japanese fast-food *sushi* restaurant called *kaitenzushi*, in which plates of *sushi* circulate on a conveyor belt in front of diners seated at a counter. The westernized version of *kaitenzushi* is a circular moat filled with a stream of flowing water. *Sushi* chefs prepare large batches of *sushi* at a prep station in the middle of the moat and place individual plates of *sushi* on a procession of little flat-bottomed wooden boats that float along in the moat. Diners sit at a low counter on the outer side of the moat and help themselves to the plates of *sushi* as they float by. When you're finished, the waitress tallies up the bill by counting the empty plates and beverage bottles. This is an especially easy way for novices to try a variety of *sushi* in a relaxed, low-pressure environment. You choose only those dishes that look appetizing, and you have the opportunity to ask questions about the exotic ones. 🦐

Placing Your Order

Those *sushi* veterans who have already experienced and enjoyed the pleasures of this exquisite edible art are probably right at home when they visit their favorite *sushi* bar. But for *sushi* novices, the first experience can be a little intimidating.

The most important thing to remember is that the proprietor and staff are happy that you have chosen to visit their establishment. "*Irasshai mase!*" the greeting they probably regaled you with when you walked through the door means, "Welcome! Come on in!" So there's no need to feel timid or shy. What's more, it's okay to let them know that it's your first visit to a *sushi* bar, or that you're still getting acquainted with Japanese cuisine.

The best seat in the house is the one with a clear view of the display case and the *sushi* chef's prep station. There you will be able to inspect the quality of the day's seafood offerings and enjoy a bird's eye view of the master plying his craft. You'll also have the chef nearby whenever you wish to order another *sushi* delicacy.

Once you're seated, the first thing you'll be served are an *oshibori* and *agari* – a warm towel and a steaming mug of green tea. You might also be treated to a tiny complimentary appetizer such as thinly sliced cucumbers and minced octopus in rice vinegar and sesame oil. None of these items will appear on your bill.

The sole responsibility of the *sushi* chef is making *sushi*, so that's the only thing you should order from him. All other items should be ordered from the servers who circulate around the dining room and the perimeter of the *sushi* bar; it is their function to provide beverages, food from the kitchen, refills, extra condiments, and the bill at the end of the meal.

When the server stops by for the first time to greet you and pour your tea, you can also order another beverage such as beer or *sake* if you wish, as well as nibbles such as *edamame* (soybeans in the pod), or a bowl of *miso* soup. These light starters will tide you over while you decide on your *sushi* choices and wait for the chef to prepare them.

Once you're settled in, it's time to turn your attention to *sushi*. You will probably be given a menu with a list of all the types of *sushi* offered, or perhaps there will be a laminated picture menu of all the *sushi* basics from which you can choose. On a chalkboard behind the chef, you may also find a list of seasonal items or house specialties, such as combination plates or elaborate *makizushi* rolls.

For ordering *sushi*, there are two Japanese expressions: *O-makase*, which means that you trust the chef to serve you what he thinks is best; and *O-konomi*, which means you'd like to choose for yourself.

If you reply with *O-makase*, the chef may ask if there is anything that you dislike, so that he will know what items to leave off your order. If you reply with *O-konomi*, you can still ask the chef for his recommendations from among what's available that day. Of course, it isn't necessary to speak Japanese. This can all be transacted in English.

One of the best choices for a *sushi* beginner is a combination plate. Many *sushi* bars offer several choices, which vary according to the cost and 'exotica' of the ingredients. Most *sushi* bars that offer such combination plates include a basic assortment of the most popular and palatable favorites, as well as combinations of 'acquired taste' items. If you choose a combination plate that includes something you aren't keen to try, such as eel or roe, you may request that the chef substitute something of equal value but more to your liking.

A perfect choice for a *sushi* tyro would be to start with a steaming bowl of *miso* soup, followed by an order of *sashimi*, perhaps *maguro*, *hamachi* and *sake* (slices of raw tuna, yellowtail and salmon). Next you might enjoy one pair each of *nigiri maguro*, *tai*, and *ebi* (slices of tuna, snapper, and steamed shrimp atop pads of vinegared rice). Follow those with an order of *sushimaki*, such as California roll, or one of the house specialties such as Spider roll, made with fried soft-shell crab.

And just for the sake of adventure, you might like to try an order of *tako*, *unagi*, or *tobiko* (octopus, toasted freshwater eel, or the tiny orange roe of the flying fish). For a taste of something lightly sweet at the end of the meal, you might enjoy an order of *tamago*, a delicate egg omelet atop a pad of rice. Or the chef may offer a selection of fresh fruit with a splash of *sake*.

When ordering from the chef at the *sushi* bar, it's important to relax and pace yourself. Order only one or two items at a time, and once they're served, savor each one slowly, taking the time to appreciate its beauty and subtlety.

For dining *a la carte*, there is no prescribed sequence for ordering and eating the *sushi* you select. But because of its delicate subtlety, *sashimi* should always be enjoyed first, and the consensus for optimum enjoyment of other items is light to heavy, mild to strong or spicy, and savory to sweet. Ultimately... the choice is yours. 🦐

Sushi Etiquette

A *sushi* meal is one of the world's most refined and exquisite dining experiences, but its pleasures do not come without a price—etiquette. The Japanese people have rules of etiquette for every aspect of life, and *sushi* is no exception. And while the list of *sushi* dos and don'ts may seem daunting at first, after a few visits to your favorite *sushi* bar, they will become second nature.

Upon Arrival

When greeted by the chef and his staff with a chorus of "*Irasshai mase!*" respond with a friendly hello, or even better, "*Konban-wa*" if it's evening, or "*Konnichi-wa*" if it's daytime.

You needn't remove your shoes, unless you are seated on the floor in a *tatami* room. If so, leave your socks on, and place your shoes neatly together on the *genkan* with toes pointed outward toward the door.

When the server brings the *oshibori* towel, which may be steaming hot in the winter and chilled in the summer, use it for cleaning your hands only. Do not wipe your face with it. When finished, fold it neatly and place it back in its dish or

Northern Lights Library System
Postal Bag 8
Elk Point Alberta
T0A 1A0

basket. And do not use it to mop up spills during the meal, and do not use it as a napkin. You will be provided with a paper or cloth napkin for wiping your fingers and mouth throughout the meal.

Ordering

If you sit at a table or in a *tatami* room, you should order everything from the server. However, if you sit at the *sushi* bar, you should order only *sushi* from the *sushi* chef, and everything else from the server, including beverages, food from the kitchen, refills, extra condiments, and the bill at the end of the meal.

The *sushi* bar is intended for the enjoyment of *sushi*, so if you wish to order a full-course meal of hot food from the kitchen, you should sit at a table in the dining room.

Don't order too much *sushi* from the chef at one time. *Sushi* is meant to be a leisurely experience that progresses throughout the evening. Remember that the chef is preparing food for everyone in the restaurant. Ordering a little at a time also ensures that you will not order too much and end up leaving it unfinished.

Chopstick Etiquette

If you don't already know how to use chopsticks, it's recommended that you brush up on your technique before your first visit to a *sushi* bar. The chopsticks will probably arrive in a little paper sleeve, still attached to each other at the upper end. When you break them apart, if you are concerned about splinters, you can rub the chopsticks against each other to hone any rough edges. However, be forewarned that doing so may be taken as an insult that the chopsticks are of inferior quality. So do so at your own discretion.

There are a number of dos and don'ts associated with chopsticks. Most importantly, never poke them into a dish of food and leave them standing upright. This is the ultimate *faux pas*. Offerings of food with chopsticks standing upright in them are presented to the spirits of the dead at funerals and gravesites, and to do so among the living is strictly taboo.

And that's not all. You should never point or otherwise gesticulate with chopsticks. They should never be used to spear a morsel of food, and the end of the chopstick that has been in your mouth should never be used to take food from a shared plate. When helping yourself from a shared dish, turn the chopsticks around and use the upper end to pick up a bite and put it on your own plate. And while you're at it, don't hover over the dish, playing eenie-meenie-minee-mo with your chopsticks. Choose your bite with your eyes and go directly for it.

Never lick your chopsticks. Don't use them to move dishes or plates. Don't make noise by hitting your plates or glasses with your chopsticks. And when not in use, they should be placed parallel to the edge of the *sushi* bar, either resting across your soy sauce dish, or with the tips on the *hashi oki* chopstick rest, if one is provided. Never put your chopsticks directly on the *sushi* bar, or leave them resting on a communal dish.

And as if that weren't enough, food should also never be passed from one set of chopsticks to another, because it is reminiscent of a ritual practiced at funerals in which the charred remains of the deceased are transferred from the crematory chamber to the burial urn by passing them from person to person using chopsticks. It's also bad form to feed someone else with your chopsticks. A typical *sushi* meal comes with all sorts of little individual dishes that are perfect for sharing food. When it comes to chopsticks, if you want to stay out of trouble, the best rule of thumb is never to let them stray from the short and narrow path between your plate and your mouth.

Soy Sauce

A small ceramic dish will be included at your place setting for holding soy sauce, which is provided in small carafes on the *sushi* bar. You may help yourself to soy sauce throughout the meal, taking care not to spill as you pour it into the dish. Many soy bottles have two small holes in the top. If you put your finger over one of the holes as you pour, and then gently lift it to allow a little air inside, you can control the flow of soy sauce. You should only pour enough soy sauce into the dish to barely cover the bottom so that the *sushi* doesn't become saturated with it when you dip it.

If you like *wasabi*, it is okay to mix a little with your soy sauce. But don't overdo it. Not only is it considered a breach of etiquette, but too much *wasabi* will overpower the delicate flavors of the *sushi*.

When dipping a piece of *sushi* into the soy sauce, it should be rotated so that only the fish touches the soy sauce. Otherwise, the rice will disintegrate and make a mess in the dish. And it is considered rude to leave a dish full of rice at the end of the meal.

If a piece of *sushi* already has some kind of sauce on it, such as *unagi*, or one of the house specialty *makizushi* rolls, it should not be dipped in soy sauce.

Eating *Sushi*

Picking up *sushi* with your fingers is the traditional method of eating *sushi* in Japan, and is perfectly acceptable, although the use of chopsticks has become the preferred method for eating *sushi* in the U.S. If using your fingers, do so delicately, using only the thumb, index and middle fingers.

Most *sushi* comes in bite-sized pieces. However, some items on the menu are larger than others, and some *sushi* bars can be quite generous with their portions. Therefore, you may occasionally find yourself faced with something that won't fit comfortably in your mouth. In this event, it's okay to take a partial bite, but be forewarned that a delicate piece of *sushi* may fall apart in the process, causing the two-fold embarrassment of making a big mess on the *sushi* bar, and the awkwardness of salvaging the remnants of the remaining bite. So, when faced with a two-bite morsel, you may want to deviate from propriety and pick up that piece with your fingers instead of using your chopsticks. You'll have much more control over its structural integrity that way. Whatever you do, don't put a half-eaten piece of *sushi* back on your plate. Hold onto it until you're ready to finish it.

Another thing to consider is that some seafoods, such as squid, octopus, and large clams, are not easy to bite in half. With those, you'll have to bite the bullet, so to speak, and put the whole thing in your mouth at once. But if you do decide to go for the whole thing, it's not only polite, but also customary to shield your mouth from view with your free hand until you've wrestled the mega-bite into submission. It is also acceptable to ask the chef to cut larger pieces of *sushi* in half. And *sashimi* should always be eaten with chopsticks, not your fingers.

Miso soup is meant to be sipped from the bowl in which it is served. Holding your chopsticks in one hand and the soup bowl in the other, sip the broth directly from the bowl and use your chopsticks to eat the *tofu* and seaweed floating in the soup. And unlike western etiquette, in Japan, it's perfectly acceptable to make a small slurping sound when you sip the soup, especially if it's very hot.

The pickled ginger that goes with *sushi* is intended as a condiment, a palate refresher to be nibbled between bites. It is not a salad or a side dish, so don't overdo it. However, if you do run out of ginger before you finish your order of *sushi*, it's fine to request a little more, either from the chef or from your server.

Beverages

When dining with a companion or a group, it is customary in Japan to pour beverages for each other. Your server may pour the first serving into your glass, but thereafter, it is polite to keep your companion's glass filled and to hold your glass toward other people when they offer to pour for you.

If you are dining late, it is considered polite to offer the *sushi* chef a drink of either *sake* or beer. Simply order a bottle or carafe from your server, request two glasses or cups, and pour one for the chef. A drink for the chef is not typically offered at lunchtime.

The traditional Japanese expression for raising a toast is "*Kampai*!" It means "Empty the glass!"

Table Manners

Don't rest your elbows on a table when eating. It is considered impolite in both Japan and the U.S.

Ask for a fork or spoon if you cannot use chopsticks. But don't ask for a knife because it may be taken as an insult that the food is tough.

Try to eat all the dishes evenly. Don't eat just one dish until it is empty.

Try to eat everything you order. It is considered rude to leave food on your plate, especially rice.

As a courtesy to others, never smoke in a *sushi* bar.

At the End of the Meal

When you are finished ordering *sushi*, place your chopsticks across your soy saucer, parallel to the edge of the *sushi* bar. This will signal to the chef and your server that you are finished. Do not leave your chopsticks on the *sushi* bar or on a serving plate.

When you are ready to leave, ask your server for the bill. Do not ask the chef, since it is customary in Japan that those who prepare food do not handle money.

Tipping is not customary in Japan; however, it is expected in *sushi* bars in the U.S. While some believe that the chef and server should be tipped separately, it is also fine to leave a communal tip for both. Just be sure it's a generous one. 🎴

Sushi Lingo and Conversational Phrases

As in any language, please and thank you are the first best words to learn. In Japanese, please is *kudasai*, and thank you is *arigato*. Learning the Japanese names for all the items on the *sushi* menu is also useful, but if you dare, there are many other phrases that will go a long way toward enhancing the enjoyment of your *sushi* experience. Here are a few of the most common ones:

Good afternoon. – Konnichi-wa.

Good evening. – Konban-wa.

How are you? – O-genki desu ka?

I'm fine. – Genki desu.

How's it going? – Ikaga desu ka?

Everything's fine. – Ii desu.

It's hot. – Atsui desu.

It's cold. – Samui desu.

It's busy, isn't it? – Isogashi desu, ne?

Beer please. – Biru o kudasai.

Sake please. – O-sake o kudasai.

Large please. – Oki kudasai.

Small please. – Chisai kudasai.

Cheers! – Kampai. (A toast that means "Empty the glass.")

Chef – Itamae-san.

What is your name? – Anata no namae wa?

My name is Joe. – Namae wa Joe desu.

Please choose for me. – Omakase ni shite kudasai.

Please take what is offered. – Dozo.

Thanks. – Domo.

Thank you. – Arigato.

Thank you very much. – Domo arigato gozaimasu.

Sashimi please. – Sashimi o kudasai.

I gratefully receive (as a blessing or grace before eating). – Itadakimasu.

Yes. – Hai.

No. – Iie.

Just a little please. – Sukoshi dake kudasai.

A little more please. – Mo sukoshi kudasai.

It's just right! Perfect! – Chodo ii desu.

It looks delicious! – Oishiso.

It's delicious! – Oishi desu!

I like it! – Suki desu.

You're very skillful! – Jozu desu!

I'm full. – Ipai desu.

That's all for now, thank you. – Mo kekko desu.

Thank you very much (at the end of the meal). – Arigato gozaimashita.

It was a feast. (As an expression of thanks after a meal.) – Gochiso-sama.

My bill please. – Okanjo onegai shimasu. (Oaiso onegai shimasu is another way to ask for the check)

It was wonderful! – Yokatta desu!

Good night. – Oyasumi nasai.

Slang Terms
Gyoku – A slang term for *tamago*, egg omelet. It literally
means jewel.

Murasaki – A slang term for soy sauce. It literally means purple.

Namida – A slang term for *wasabi*. It literally means tears.

Sushi Counting Jargons
The Japanese people use a complex method of counting, which
involves the addition of a suffix after the basic number that
tells what kind of item is being counted, usually related to the
shape or size of the object. The numbers from one to ten are
ichi, ni, san, shi (yon), go, roku, shichi (nana), hachi, ku, ju. The
words for four and seven also sound the same as the word for
death, so in superstitious tradition, the words *yon* and *nana* are
substituted. And in counting, *hito* and *futa* are often substituted
for one and two. For counting *sushi*, the suffix is *–kan*. So counting
pieces of *sushi* goes *hito-kan, futa-kan, san-kan*, etc.

There is also a special slang lingo for the all the numbers as well.
These terms vary widely according to region and individual
establishments and are often used as a secret code so that their
patrons' orders and bill totals may be discussed among the staff
without seeming indiscreet. 🦐

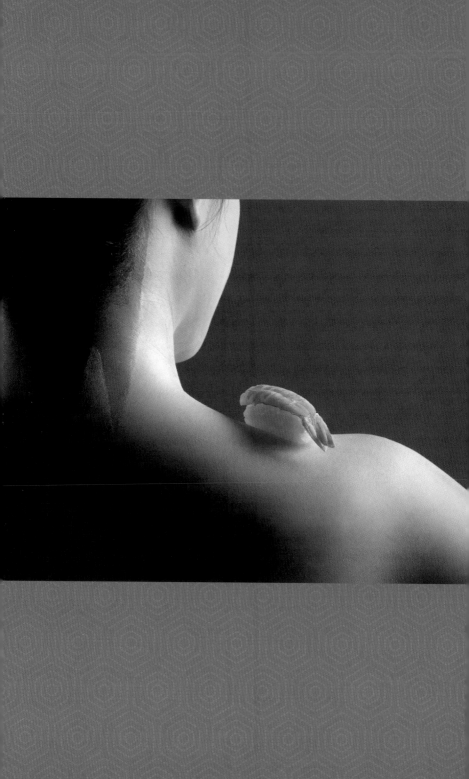

Extreme *Sushi*

Gold-Leaf *Sushi*

As if *sushi* weren't expensive enough already, imagine how a few flakes of 24-carat gold leaf might up the stakes. Gold is biologically inert, which means that it cannot be absorbed, digested, or metabolized by the human body, and therefore it is perfectly safe to eat. A box of 25 whisper-thin gold leaves or a .35 g. (.01 oz.) shaker of gold flakes will cost only about $25 U.S. at gourmet culinary supply stores. A little gold goes a long way toward enhancing the cachet of an upscale *sushi* restaurant.

Dancing Shrimp

Sushi doesn't come any fresher than *odori ebi*, dancing shrimp, served live and consumed still wriggling. In the now-antiquated 1969 Time-Life book *The Cooking of Japan*, author Rafael Steinberg vividly describes his first and only encounter with *odori ebi*:

"A Japanese doctor I know introduced me to *odori* at a an excellent but unpretentious restaurant in the Shinjuku section of Tokyo. We sat at a counter and sipped *sake*. Then my host said something to the chef. Before my eyes the chef grabbed a live shrimp from a squirming tankful, gutted and beheaded it with two quick flicks of his knife, stripped off the shell and rinsed the flesh, and placed the dancing shrimp in front of me—all in about five seconds. Before I could react, he did the same with another for my friend, who immediately captured it by the wriggling tail, dipped it in a sauce, and swallowed it down, adding appreciative sounds.

"Determined not to be outfaced, I summoned all my resolve and reached for mine, but it squirmed violently—in agony, I was sure—and escaped from my trembling fingers. That was enough for this adventurous American. I waited patiently until the performance was over and then gingerly tasted the shrimp. It was delicious, of course, although my host told me I had missed the best part. He insisted that the flavor is several times better while the *odori* is in progress—and I am willing to take his word for it."

Live Masterpiece

Shrimp isn't the only item that is sometimes served still moving. A dish called *ikezukuri* is a whole, live fish with its mid-section filleted, sliced into *sashimi*, and reassembled on the serving dish.

The literal translation of *ikezukuri* is "live masterpiece," and any chef who prepares it must be highly skilled. When a customer orders it, a live fish is selected from a fish tank. The chef pins the fish to a cutting board, fillets the meat from one side, slices it into *sashimi*, sets it back into place, garnishes it with seaweed, arranges the fish in a curved pose on the plate using special pin blocks, and serves it, still quivering, to the customer. Fish for *ikezukuri* include sea bream and other small fish.

Ikezukuri is not for the squeamish or faint of heart, and has been banned in certain places outside Japan.

Fugu

Fugu is the Japanese name for the blowfish, also known as globefish, or puffer fish. This much-maligned delicacy is a seasonal rarity in Japan, and even more so in *sushi* bars outside Japan. According to the experts, not only is this fish a tasty treat for the palate, but consuming it comes with a certain element of risk.

The liver, ovaries and eggs of the *fugu* contain a powerful toxin, which, when inexpertly handled, imparts a deadly poison. But in the hands of a skilled *sushi* chef, the liver can be nicked to impart just enough of its toxin to numb the lips and produce a mildly euphoric effect. Try it at your own risk, and always under the guidance of a reputable *fugu* master.

Much of the *fugu* served as *sashimi* is cultivated in commercial fish farms in the city of Shimonoseki in the province of Yamaguchi at the southeastern tip of Japan's largest island, where a single *fugu* fish can cost the equivalent of $150. There are approximately 40 different varieties of *fugu*, and 10,000 tons of the deadly delicacies are consumed each year.

Should you decide to take the plunge, it would be wise to follow a few guidelines. Choose an establishment that specializes in *fugu* and call ahead for a reservation. Be prepared to pay as much as $200 per person for a *fugu* meal, and sit at the bar so that you can watch the preparation process. Order only *fugu*, as it is a unique delicacy to be savored all by itself, and the portions are usually generous enough to satisfy the average appetite.

Fugu dishes include *fugu-sashi*, thinly sliced raw *fugu* with *ponzu*, a citrus-soy dipping sauce; *fugu-chiri*, vegetables and *fugu* simmered in seaweed broth with *ponzu* dipping sauce; *fugu kara-age*, floured and deep fried; and *fugu hire-zake*, grilled *fugu* fin steeped in hot *sake*.

The presentation of *fugu-sashi* is quite elaborate and decorative, with the translucent slices of fish and a few slivers of the skin arranged on a plate in the shape of flowers, birds or fish. *Fugu* is typically served with thinly sliced green onions, grated *daikon* radish, a wedge of Japanese lime called *sudachi*, and *ponzu* for dipping. A fine *sake* is the perfect beverage to complement *fugu*.

Fugu should be eaten very slowly, not only for the full appreciation of its subtle flavor and texture, but also as a safety precaution. As you eat *fugu*, you may notice a slight tingling sensation in your tongue and lips. If at anytime they become numb, stop eating and seek medical help immediately. In case you don't fully comprehend the risks involved, a Japanese expression sums it up: "Last night, I ate *fugu* with him... Today I help carry his coffin."

Naked *Sushi*

A longstanding tradition that dates back to feudal Japan, *nyotaimori* is the presentation of *sushi*, served up on the body of a naked woman. Contrary to popular belief, this culinary custom is as rare but not unheard of in Japan as it is elusive in other countries. Many catering companies now offer *nyotaimori* as a novelty for private parties, and some bold public establishments have cashed in on its sensationalistic appeal as a means to bolster business. The most widely publicized *nyotaimori* venue was Seattle's Bonzai, where a modest cover charge and the purchase of a cocktail entitled its patrons to four pieces of *sushi*, selected from an assortment arranged on the naked body of a comely young model. The concept was wildly popular, with patrons standing in long lines to enjoy the novel experience; however, Bonzai's *nyotaimori* nights raised such controversy among conservatives, feminists, and human rights activists that they have since discontinued the weekly event.

Nyotaimori literally means "woman body serving," and for such events, the featured woman is bathed, denuded and her torso wrapped in plastic film to ensure that her skin does not actually come into contact with the food. Guests are required to use chopsticks in helping themselves to the exotic fare that adorns her otherwise naked body. 🦐

How To Tell If a *Sushi* Bar Is Good or Bad

The quality of *sushi* bars varies widely, from mass-produced, all-you-can-eat buffets, to exclusive, world-class establishments where a single meal may cost upwards of $500 per person. Most fall somewhere in between.

The best indicators of a good *sushi* bar are a clean, tastefully appointed room filled with a pleasant aroma, an attractive display case of conspicuously fresh seafood, a mature, competent and friendly *itamae-san* behind the bar, limited seating that is full to overflowing every day, with lots of Japanese customers among its clientele.

Things to beware of, although not always indicators of sub-standard quality, are all-you-can-eat *sushi* buffets, franchise establishments, conveyor belt or water moat *sushi*, a menu that does not specialize exclusively in Japanese cuisine, and an absence of Japanese employees among the staff. That being said, there are certainly many exceptions to these caveats. My very favorite *sushi* bar in all the world, mostly for sentimental reasons, is Isobune, the water-moat establishment in San Francisco's Japantown where I had my first *sushi* experience. And my favorite local *sushi* bar, a place called Sushi Mambo, is owned and operated by two brothers from Mexico, both of whom are highly trained and extremely competent *itamae-san*.

The best litmus test of quality is your own power of observation. When you arrive, take a look around. Is the place clean and fragrant? Is the *itamae-san* pleasant and crisply dressed, behind a clean, organized and uncluttered chef's station? Is the display case filled with a wide variety of appetizing seafood? Is the place busy and lively? Were you greeted in a friendly manner when you walked in the door? If your answer to these questions is "Yes," then chances are, a delightful *sushi* experience awaits you.

Or…is the display case sparsely stocked and smudged with fingerprints? Is the *sushi* bar sticky or littered with unbussed dishes? Does the place smell of fish? Is the chef's station messy and haphazardly arranged? Is the *itamae-san* absent, or languishing behind the bar? Are the seats empty at a time when you'd expect most places to be full? If so, don't even bother sitting down. Chances are you will be disappointed.

And even if your first impression is favorable, there are other telltale signs of sub-standard quality. A questionable establishment may have no display case, or a sparsely stocked case of dry or discolored seafood, a limited number of raw fish selections with most of the menu consisting of combination rolls or cooked items, a menu with no Japanese words on it, a chef who does not know the Japanese names of the *sushi*, or one who expects you to order all your *sushi* at once.

Expensive prices are not always a guarantee of quality, however. If the prices look too good to be true, then chances are it will be reflected in the quality of the *sushi* and the service. So, when choosing a *sushi* bar, especially for your first *sushi* experience, ask around for recommendations and visit the best establishment you can afford. 🦐

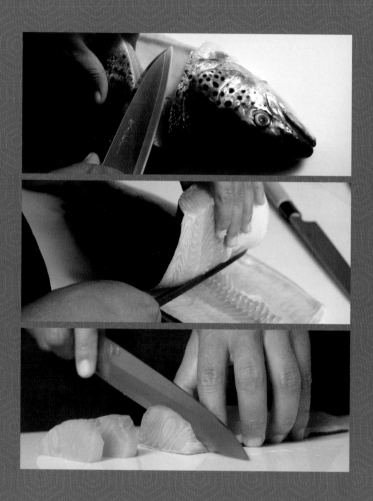

The Fish Market

Every coastal city has its own fish market where local fishermen sell the catch of the day, while inland cities must rely on air transport to deliver *sushi*-grade seafood, whether fresh or frozen. Large coastal cities such as New York, San Francisco, Los Angeles, Hong Kong, Shanghai, Singapore, Bangkok, Manila, Jakarta, Bombay, Sydney, Athens, Capetown, Panama, Vancouver, Buenos Aries, and Rio de Janiero have bustling emporiums frequented by local wholesalers, retailers, chefs and restaurateurs who rise with the sun each day to procure the freshest best for their seafood dishes. But none is so famed for the fish that will be transformed into *sushi* as Tokyo's Tsukuji Fish Market.

Located on the Hibiya Subway Line near Tokyo's Ginza district, just a few blocks from the Sumida River, the Tsukiji Fish Market has a long and tumultuous history that dates back to feudal times. Originally located in Nihonbashi, near the bridge for which the district is named, the fish market was stocked with the overflow of seafood from purveyors to Edo Castle, the stronghold of the great *shogun* Ieyasu Tokugawa.

After the Great Fire of 1657, which killed nearly 100,000 people and leveled the city surrounding the castle grounds, the *shogun*, undaunted by the disaster, decreed that Edo would be rebuilt, much of it on land that had once been the eastern marshes. This district was named *Tsukiji*, which means reclaimed land, and later became the home of Japan's naval training academy, as well as a foreign settlement for diplomats, missionaries, and teachers who arrived as Japan opened its doors to the world at the dawn of the Meiji Era. However, when the Great Kanto Earthquake of 1923 struck, destroying much of downtown Tokyo, the fish market was relocated from Nihonbashi to the same site that had once been the naval academy in Tsukiji.

Today, the facility covers more than 50 acres (20 hectares), occupied by more than a thousand vendors, and is surrounded by a complex network of streets and alleyways lined with shops selling knives and other culinary wares, specialty ingredients, and best of all, the very freshest *sushi* to be found anywhere on planet earth.

Tsukiji Fish Market comes to life each morning between the hours of midnight and 4 a.m., when trucks bearing loads of every imaginable variety of marine creature arrive to make their deliveries. Soon, wholesalers begin arriving to inspect the day's catch, and at precisely 5:20 a.m., the fish auctions begin. In a fast and furious language all their own, the fish dealers and wholesalers negotiate their transactions, claim their purchases, and in a matter of minutes, the show is over.

Next come the retailers. From 6:00 to 9:00 a.m., chefs, restaurateurs, and the proprietors of neighborhood seafood markets come to buy their bounty for the day. By 10 a.m., the Tsukiji Fish Market, which just minutes before had bustled with more than 15,000 workers and untold numbers of visitors, is now virtually empty. Many of them have headed off to their businesses, while others enjoy a much-needed respite over lunch at one of the dozens of *sushi* bars and restaurants in the surrounding neighborhood.

Tsukiji Fish Market is not for everyone, but if you're hardy enough to brave the streets of downtown Tokyo in the middle of the night to stand in puddles of water as throngs of fish merchants scuffle to and fro with barrows full of fish, then you're in for a spectacle that few tourists have ever witnessed. 魚

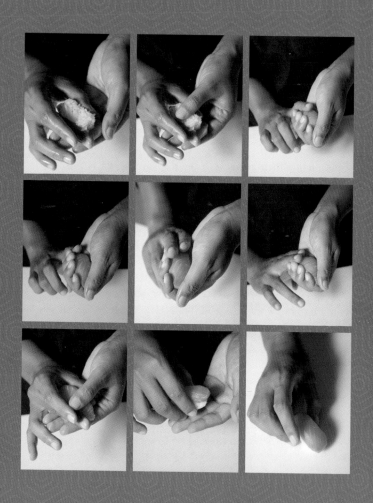

Wasabi

Becoming a *Sushi* Chef

Although there is a year-long course for those who wish to learn the basics offered at the Sushi Academy in the Tokyo suburb of Sugamo, the process of becoming a licensed *sushi* chef requires a much lengthier apprenticeship as a *minarai*. The practice of apprenticeship is a longstanding tradition in Japan, where it is believed that only through years of repetition and rigorous training under the scrutiny of a master, will an apprentice learn to appreciate the deeper meaning and honor of the profession, as well as the development of skills necessary to carry it out to perfection.

An aspiring *itamae-san* usually begins his apprenticeship of ten years or more as a dishwasher and general assistant to the *shokunin*, the *sushi* master. In the process, the *minarai* learns by observation, all the ingredients, recipes, and preparation techniques, as well as the general operation of the establishment. However, he must spend several years observing and helping out around the *sushi* shop before he will be allowed to touch a knife.

The apprenticeship of a *minarai* is an especially stringent one. Not only must he learn to slice fish precisely and perfectly each time, he must also know how to select the best seafood, how to handle and store it properly, how to prepare all the sauces and garnishes, how to keep an accurate running tally of orders in his head, and how to cater to the likes and dislikes of his regular patrons.

With its beginnings in the *samurai* tradition, the status of *shokunin* is a noble and highly respected one that takes many years to achieve. A *shokunin* is a man of impeccable standards and unimpeachable discipline. However, you may be surprised to learn that even the best *itamae-san* in the U.S. might not be considered qualified to call themselves *shokunin* in Japan. Many *itamae-san* who prepare *sushi* in the U.S. are individuals who have abandoned their apprenticeships before completion to seek their freedom and fortune in a burgeoning new market where their already-superior skills are in great demand. 🦋

Wasabi

Ko

Famous *Sushi* Bars

According to the latest tally on The *Sushi* World Guide website, which appears to be the world's most comprehensive and current database of *sushi* bars outside Japan, there are approximately 4000 *sushi* restaurants in more than 1000 cities worldwide. The Munich-based site is the vision-come-true of freelance director and world-traveling *sushi* lover Michael Bentele, and web designer Sebastian Schnitzenbaumer. By virtue of their excellent *sushi* search engine, it seems that no matter where in the world you go, you'll probably be able to find a *sushi* restaurant somewhere nearby. Here's the URL to the Sushi World Guide website: **http://www.sushi.infogate.de/index.shtml**. And while the restaurants it contains are far too numerous to list here, these are some of the most famous.

Tokyo
Ginza Kyubei
Japan's most famous and reputable *sushi* restaurant, established in 1936 by *itamae-san* and potter Kitaoji Rosanjin, whose *sushi* creations were served on his own handmade dishes, which are still available upon request. Ginza Kyubei is also credited with inventing *gunkan sushi*, or 'battleship' style, in which a narrow strip of *nori* extends slightly beyond the top of the ball of

vinegared rice, creating a shallow niche to hold a small serving of a soft ingredient such as fish roe, sea urchin, or minced shellfish.

Ginza Kyubei
7-6, Ginza 8-chome
Chuo-ku, Tokyo
Phone: 03-3571-6523

Flavio Parisi

Maguro-bito

The most popular *kaiten-zushi* shop in Tokyo, where plates of *sushi* roll past on a conveyor belt.

Maguro-bito
5-9, Asakusa 1-chome
Taito-ku, Tokyo
Phone: 03-3844-8736

Emily Vaughn

Osaka

Kodai Suzume-zushi Sushiman

The oldest *sushi* restaurant in Japan, established in 1653 as a fish market, now known for its Osaka-style pressed sea bream *sushi*.

Kodai Suzume-zushi Sushiman
5-11, Koraibashi 4-chome,
Chuo-ku, Osaka
Phone: 06-6231-1520

Nobu

With his upscale restaurants popping up all over the globe, Chef Nobuyuki Matsuhisa is taking the *sushi* world by storm, and even among *sushi* beginners, his name will soon be a household word.

Nobu Tokyo
6-10-1 Minami Aoyama
Minato-ku, Tokyo 107-0062
Phone: 81-3-5467-0022

Nobu New York
105 Hudson Street
New York, NY 10013
Phone: 212-219-0500

Next Door Nobu
105 Hudson Street
New York, NY 10013
Phone: 212-219-0500

Nobu 57th Street
40 West 57th Street
New York, NY 10019
Phone: 212-757-3000

Nobu Milan (Inside the Armani Store)
Alia SRL
Via Manzoni 31
Milan, Italy 20121
Phone: 39-02-723-18645

Nobu London
19 Old Park Lane
London, England W1Y 4LB
Phone: 44-207-447-4747

Camilla Hacking

Nobu Berkeley
15 Berkeley Street
London, England W1J 8DY
Phone: 44-207-290-9222

Camilla Hacking

Nobu Malibu
3835 Cross Creek Road
Malibu, CA 90265 Malibu
Phone: 310-317-9140

Nobu Las Vegas
Hard Rock Hotel
4455 Paradise Road
Las Vegas, NV 89109
Phone: 702-693-5090

Nobu Dallas
400 Crescent Court
Dallas, TX 75201
Phone:214-252-7000

Singapore
Sakae Sushi
Its name means 'growth' in Japanese, and rightfully so with Sakae's more than 15 locations in Singapore, and additional branches in Thailand, Indonesia, China and Malaysia. The original Sakae Sushi, at Singapore's OUB Center, features the world's longest conveyor belt *sushi* bar at 129 m. (423 ft.).

Sakae Sushi
1 Raffles Place
B1-07/08 OUB Centre,
Singapore 048616
Phone: 6438-6281

London
Yo! Sushi
Any Internet keyword search for '*sushi*' will undoubtedly yield a mention of London's Yo! Sushi, a *kaiten-zushi* style restaurant that features one of the world's longest *sushi* conveyor belts at 60 m. (197 ft.). Yo! Sushi also has branches in Finchley, Oxford Street, Harvey Nichols, Selfridges and MyHotel.

Yo! Sushi
52 Poland Street, W1
London, England W1F 7NH
Phone: 020-7287 0443

Maya Hart

Preparing a *Sushi* Dinner at Home

Although it may lack the exotic ambiance of a visit to your favorite *sushi* bar, preparing a *sushi* dinner at home can be a very rewarding and enlightening experience. Not only will it fill you with a sense of pride and accomplishment, it will give you a renewed respect for the *itamae-san* who prepares your *sushi* when you dine out.

What follows here is a recommendation for a basic but authentic, elegant and satisfying *sushi* meal, including everything from snacks to nibble while you put the finishing touches on the main course, to a light, refreshing dessert to enjoy afterwards.

Snacks

Enjoying a variety of bite-sized foods over cold beers and hot *sake* is one of the best ways to relax in the company of friends and family. Japanese appetizers run the gamut from blanched soybeans called *edamame*, and crunchy rice crackers called *sembei*, to simple steamed shellfish, tiny deep-fried river shrimp, and *tofu* cubes with soy sauce and bonito flakes.

Any well-stocked gourmet grocery or Asian market, especially one that specializes in Japanese foods, will carry a variety of *sembei* snacks. These crunchy little rice crackers and tidbits are usually seasoned with soy sauce, some are wrapped in *nori*, and all are delicious. However, beware that many contain MSG, so read the labels if you're sensitive or allergic. *Sembei* make an excellent starter for you and your guests to munch on while finishing up with the preparations. They are especially tasty with a nice, cold Japanese beer.

Edamame

These tasty young soybean pods are most commonly available in the frozen vegetable section of some supermarkets and many Asian grocery stores. To prepare, follow the cooking instructions on the package.

If you are fortunate enough to find them fresh at a produce market in the late summer months, or you are able to grow your own, remove the fresh pods from the beanstalk, wash them thoroughly and drop them in boiling water for about five minutes, or until tender. When they're done, remove them from the water, drain them and sprinkle lightly with coarse salt if you like. Allow them to cool and serve them in the pods.

Edamame can also be prepared in the microwave. Place 2 cups (473 ml.) of soybean pods in a microwave-safe dish, cover and cook on full power for 4 or 5 minutes. Sprinkle lightly with coarse salt, allow them to cool and serve in their pods.

Green Tea

The green tea that the Japanese people drink on a daily basis is quite different from the tea used in the Japanese Tea Ceremony. *Ocha*, or *agari* as it is called in *sushi* bars, is made from loose dried tea leaves, which are available in several grades, while tea ceremony tea is an intensely flavorful powdered tea that makes a frothy foam when whisked in hot water. Here's how to make a pot of everyday *ocha*:

Japanese Green Tea (4 servings)
4 cups (946 ml.) hot water, just under boiling temperature
5 tbsp. (74 ml.) green tea leaves

Place the loose tea leaves into a teapot. Add hot water. Steep for 3 to 5 minutes. Pour into *cha-wan* mugs and serve hot.

Miso Soup

Japanese soups tend to be light and clear, made with a soup base called *dashi*. This basic stock, steeped with dried kelp and smoky dried bonito shavings, is the foundation for Japan's most popular soup, *miso shiru*, which consists of *dashi*, *miso* paste, flakes of dried *wakame* seaweed, and cubes of firm *tofu*.

Miso Soup (4 Servings)
The base for this delicious soup is a stock called *dashi*. To make *dashi*, you will need:

1 qt. (946 ml.) of water
1-4 in. (10 cm.) piece of dried *konbu* (dried sea kelp)
1 cups (237 ml.) of *katsuo* (dried bonito shavings)

Rinse or wipe the dusty coating from the surface of the *konbu* and place in a pot with 1 qt. of water and cook over high heat. When the water comes to a boil remove and discard the *konbu*. Add the *katsuo* and bring to a boil again. Remove the pan from the heat and allow it to cool. Strain the liquid into a separate container and discard the *katsuo*. The remaining liquid is called *dashi* and can be used as a base to make a wide variety of soups and dipping sauces.

To prepare *Miso* Soup you will need:
1 qt. (946 ml.) of *dashi*
4 tbsp. (59 ml.) *miso* paste
1 tbsp. (15 ml.) dried *wakame* seaweed flakes, finely chopped
1 cup (237 ml.) of *tofu* cut into 1⁄2 in. cubes

Bring the *dashi* to a boil in a large saucepan. Add the *miso* paste and stir with a wooden spoon until it dissolves completely. Bring the mixture just to a boil again and remove from the heat. Add the *tofu* cubes and *wakame*. Allow to stand for 5 minutes before serving. Ladle the soup into small bowls, stirring as you ladle to making sure that the *miso*, *tofu* cubes and *wakame* are well distributed between the portions.

Sunomono

A favorite way to begin a Japanese meal is with a light, vinegared salad made with cucumbers and other fresh vegetables, sometimes mixed with diced seafood such as crab, octopus, or shrimp and sprinkled with sesame seeds. A simple marinade of rice wine vinegar, soy sauce and a few drops of sesame oil makes an excellent dressing.

The word *sunomono* means 'vinegared things' and can be prepared with almost any combination of ingredients, from fresh raw vegetables and greens to finely diced seafoods. Here's a tasty and easy to prepare *sunomono* recipe:

(4 to 8 servings)
1 large cucumber
1 cup (237 ml.) pre-cooked bay shrimp
Rice wine vinegar dressing
Pickled ginger
Sesame seeds

Wash a large cucumber and trim off the ends. Slice the cucumber in half lengthwise and scrape out the seeds with a teaspoon. Cut the cucumber halves into paper-thin slices and place in a bowl. Add 1 cup (237 ml.) of tiny pre-cooked bay shrimp and marinate for 2 hours (stirring occasionally) in Rice Wine Vinegar Dressing:

1 cup (237 ml.) Rice Wine Vinegar
1/2 cup (118 ml.) *mirin* or *sake*
2 tbsp. (30 ml.) sesame oil

Thoroughly mix and serve the *sunomono* in small individual dishes with a slotted spoon to drain off excess marinade. Garnish with a pinch of pickled ginger and sprinkle with sesame seeds.

Sushi

Sushi, perhaps the most widely recognized of all Japanese food, is the categorical term for a variety of dishes made with vinegared rice. *Sushi* can be made with a countless array of seafoods and vegetables. Everyone has his or her own favorites. Just be sure that the ingredients you choose are absolutely the best and freshest available.

Sushi Rice (6 cups or 1.4 L.)
3 cups (710 ml.) dry white *sushi*-grade rice
3 cups (710 ml.) water
1/3 cup (79 ml.) rice wine vinegar
2 tbsp. (30 ml.) sugar
1 tsp (5 ml.) salt

Cook the rice in an automatic rice steamer, or use the stovetop instructions above. When the rice is done, dissolve the sugar and salt in the rice wine vinegar in a small pan over low heat. Sprinkle the vinegar mixture into the cooked rice and fluff gently with a wooden rice paddle to mix.

Place the cooked rice in a large wooden bowl or spread on a baking sheet to cool. Fan the rice with a pleated fan or piece of stiff paper for 8 to 10 minutes. This will produce an attractive sheen and helps keep the rice sticky. When the rice is cool to the touch, you can begin using it to make sushi.

Nigiri Sushi (About 40 Pieces)

1⁄4 lb. (.1 kg.) fresh *sushi*-grade tuna
1⁄4 lb. (.1 kg.) fresh *sushi*-grade hamachi or snapper
1⁄4 lb. (.1 kg.) smoked salmon
3 cups (710 ml.) *sushi* rice (see recipe)
2 tbsp. (30 ml.) *wasabi* paste (optional)
Pickled ginger
Soy sauce

With a very sharp knife, cut the fish into uniform 1 in. x 2 in. (2.5 cm. x 5 cm.) slices about 1⁄4 in. thick. If desired, rub a pinch of *wasabi* paste down the center of each slice.

Dip your hands in rice vinegar or warm water, and with your left hand, scoop up enough *sushi* rice to fill the center of your palm. With the index and middle fingers of your right hand, press and shape the *sushi* rice into a tight oblong ball. (You can also use a *sushi* rice mold which can be purchased in Asian markets and kitchen supply stores.)

Lay a slice of fish across the rice ball and place the *sushi* on an attractive serving dish. Repeat the process with the remaining fish and rice. Garnish with a mound of pickled ginger, a ball of *wasabi* paste and serve with soy sauce for dipping.

Tekka Maki – Tuna Rolls (24 Pieces)
2 cups (473 ml.) *sushi* rice (see recipe)
4 oz. (113 g.) fresh tuna, sliced into 1/2 in. strips
4 sheets of *nori* seaweed wrapper
1 tsp (5 ml.) *wasabi* paste
Lay a 12 in. x 12 in. (30 cm. x 30 cm.) sheet plastic of wrap on a flat dry surface, such as a cutting board or countertop. Place a sheet of *nori* on the plastic wrap.

Cover the lower half of the *nori* with a thin layer of sushi rice, pressing firmly and distributing evenly all the way out to the left and right edges.

With your right thumb, rub a pinch of *wasabi* paste on the *nori* across the top edge of the rice.

Lay several strips of tuna, end-to-end, across the center of the rice.

Moisten the upper edge of the *nori* with a few drops of water.

Starting at the bottom edge, begin firmly but gently rolling the *nori* cigar style around the strips of tuna. Continue rolling to the moistened upper edge.

Fold the plastic wrap upward around the *sushi* roll and squeeze firmly along the length of the roll to compact the filling and seal the moistened edge of the *nori*.

Remove the plastic wrap and cut the *sushi* roll into 6 uniform pieces. Repeat the process with the remaining ingredients.

Stand each set of *sushi* rolls upright on an attractive serving dish and garnish with a ball of *wasabi* paste and a mound of pickled ginger.

For variety, you can also substitute strips of fresh cucumber, smoked salmon, or imitation crab instead of the tuna filling in *makizushi*.

Seasonal Fruits in Sweet *Sake* (4 Servings)
8 large strawberries
1 navel orange
1 bunch red grapes
1 kiwi fruit
1 peach
1 cup (237 ml.) *mirin*
1 tsp (5 ml.) freshly grated ginger
1 bunch of fresh mint

Wash, peel and cut the fruits into bite-sized pieces. Place in a shallow bowl with the grated ginger and cover with *mirin*. Allow to marinate for 1 to 2 hours, stirring occasionally. Serve in small bowls with a slotted spoon and garnish with mint leaves.

Sake
Sake is traditionally served with *sashimi* at the beginning of a *sushi* meal. However, a carafe of warm *sake* is also the perfect way to end the meal as well. The best way to heat *sake* is to pour it into a *tokkuri* carafe and allow it to stand in a pan of hot water for about five minutes. You can also heat *sake* in the microwave in just 30 seconds. Be careful not to overfill the

carafe, as liquid expands when hot and may overflow the container. You can test for the perfect temperature in much the same way you might for a baby's bottle: a drop on the inner wrist, or a touch of it on the earlobe. It should be pleasantly warm but not scalding. Overheating *sake* destroys its delicate flavor and aroma.

Japanese Cooking & Serving Utensils

In a perfect world, every home kitchen would be equipped |with the finest tools and the most elegant dishware. However, preparing and serving Japanese food in your own kitchen doesn't necessarily require any expensive or esoteric utensils. The basic cookware native to the average kitchen is quite adequate for preparing most Japanese dishes. But there are special gizmos and gadgets, pots, pans and paraphernalia that do make certain tasks unique to the preparation of Japanese cuisine considerably easier, and definitely produce more professional results.

Knives

In the preparation of any type of cuisine, a quality set of knives is essential. And although Japanese knives are impressive and would lend a more authentic air to the experience of preparing a Japanese dinner, a good sharp set of domestic knives will work just as well. But keep the serrated ones in the drawer. Few if any Japanese techniques or dishes require them, and the ragged edge of a serrated blade can shred delicate seaweed wrappers.

A basic set of knives, whether Japanese or domestic, should include a large chef's knife, a smaller utility knife, a slender boning knife, a paring knife, and a cleaver. And of course, for the best results, all knives should be kept sparkling clean and razor sharp.

Pots and Pans

When compared to its sleek European counterparts, traditional Japanese cookware tends to be somewhat utilitarian. Much of it is good old-fashioned cast iron, unpretentious and indestructible. But for preparing Japanese food in your own kitchen, your garden-variety non-stick cookware will work just as well for boiling, sautéing, steaming, frying, and poaching.

The preparation of a multi-course Japanese meal may require that several dishes be cooked at once. So a basic set of cookware, whether Japanese or domestic, should include a large kettle with a tight-fitting lid, several saucepans in various sizes, a large skillet, an omelet or sauté pan, a steamer basket, and a set of non-stick baking sheets.

Other Useful Cookware

In addition to your basic pots and pans, there are many other items that will facilitate your foray into the world of Japanese cuisine. These items include:

- A large wok for frying
- Several cutting boards in various sizes
- Measuring cups and spoons for precision portions
- A large colander for rinsing and draining
- A fine sieve for straining
- A wire rack for draining
- A pair of tongs or long chopsticks for transferring food from pan to plate
- A slotted spoon for separating foods from liquids
- A basting brush for coating foods with sauces and marinades
- A fine grater for preparing condiments and garnishes

- A bamboo mat for rolling *makizushi*
- A mortar and pestle for grinding seeds and spices
- An ice pick for piercing small holes in various ingredients

There are also several modern electrical conveniences that are not essential but would certainly lend themselves to the preparation of Japanese cuisine, including an automatic rice cooker, a crock pot, a hot plate, an electric grill, and an electric deep fat fryer.

Serving Dishes

Japanese dishware, lacquerware and porcelain are among the finest in the world. But you needn't go to great lengths or extravagant expense to provide an elegant presentation for your own rendition of Japanese cuisine. The *Zen* philosophy of appreciating and utilizing whatever is at hand is the perfect attitude for serving up your culinary creations. The more rustic, the better.

Almost all Asian grocery stores carry a selection of basic plates and bowls at modest prices. Thrift shops are another good source for finding the odd Japanese dish. And if you're so inclined, you can make your own set of Japanese dishes in pottery class.

Whatever your source, to present a traditional Japanese meal for four, you will need:

- At least a dozen small, shallow dishes for condiments, dipping sauces, and appetizers
- 4-5 in. (13 cm.) half-spherical lacquer bowls for serving *miso* soup
- 4 receiving dishes for holding individual portions from shared plates
- 4 tea mugs without handles
- 4 pairs of chopsticks
- Several large serving trays

Remember that the presentation of Japanese cuisine is just as important as its preparation, and therefore, the aesthetics of your serving dishes will significantly influence the overall effect of your Japanese meal. When choosing your serving dishes, think plain, simple, elegant. Avoid bold, busy patterns, and dishes that are too large or too small for their contents.

Try to coordinate the colors of the dishes with the colors of the food, and keep in mind that many items such as baskets and colorful or interestingly textured leaves, husks, and skins that would normally be discarded might make an elegant garnish that will pull the whole dish together.

Stocking a Japanese Pantry

When making Japanese cuisine at home, simple doesn't always mean quick and easy. With all the washing, cleaning, chopping, cooking, arranging and garnishing, the preparation of many Japanese dishes can be very labor intensive. The amount of work that goes into a traditional Japanese meal is the same, whether you make it with cheap, inferior ingredients or costly top-quality ones. Therefore, it is always important to buy the freshest and very best products you can afford to ensure that your labor of love doesn't end up a big disappointment because you tried to cut corners. So don't skimp. Buy the best!

What to Keep on Hand

If you plan to make *sushi* on a regular basis, there are several items with a very long shelf life that you may want to keep on hand. Those ingredients include:

Soy sauce

A mild **soy sauce** such as Takara, or Kikkoman. Beware of cheap soy sauces, as they may tend to be thick, heavy and overly salty. Soy sauce keeps indefinitely at room temperature in a tightly sealed container.

Pickled ginger

Pickled ginger, called *gari shoga*, available in jars, bottles and occasionally in plastic containers in the produce section. Keeps indefinitely in a tightly sealed container in the refrigerator. Just be sure that the ginger is fully immersed in the rice wine vinegar.

Wasabi

Wasabi, available in prepared form in small, squeezable tubes, or in powdered form to mix with water into a soft paste. Keeps indefinitely in an airtight, bug proof container. (Believe it or not, grain moths love the stuff.)

Sesame seeds

Sesame seeds available in the spice and baking ingredients section of your grocery store. Japanese markets also carry a black, toasted variety. Will keep indefinitely in a sealed container in the refrigerator. Untoasted sesame seeds tend to go rancid at room temperature and are also a tasty target for grain moths.

Sesame oil

Sesame oil also goes rancid if left unrefrigerated, but will keep indefinitely at cooler temperatures in a tightly sealed container, although it does tend to become viscous and may need to warm up a bit before use.

Dried seaweed

Dried seaweed of all types keeps indefinitely in sealed bags or containers, but is probably best kept in the fridge to prevent unwelcome pests. Even some cats love *nori*.

Katsuo

Katsuo flakes of dried bonito will keep indefinitely in sealed bags or containers and should also be kept in the fridge just to be sure. Of course, they're so tasty and versatile, chances are they won't last long enough to spoil.

Rice wine vinegar

Rice wine vinegar will keep indefinitely at room temperature, but would best be kept in the fridge with the rest of your Japanese ingredients.

Mirin

Sweet cooking *sake*, also has an indefinite shelf life in the refrigerator.

Miso

Savory fermented soybean paste available in both red and white, does have a somewhat limited shelf life, but will keep for several months in a sealed container in the refrigerator. White *miso* is creamy and mild, while red *miso* is heavier, richer and more savory. They're virtually interchangeable in recipes, so choose according to your own taste. Beware however, that *miso* often contains MSG, so read the ingredient label if you're sensitive or allergic.

Rice

Rice can also be purchased in large quantities and stored for long periods of time. Be aware, however, that you will get the best results if you buy Japanese rice, and for making *sushi* in particular, if you purchase rice specifically intended for that purpose. Of course much of the outcome depends on the cooking process, however, *sushi* rice tends to be short-grained and therefore a little more sticky than the other varieties and holds together better for *nigiri* and *makizushi*. Do not use long-grain rice for *sushi*.

Sembei crackers

Sembei crackers are a tasty little starter for any Japanese meal. They come in dozens of varieties, from bite-sized bits and *nori*-wrapped nibbles, to large, crunchy rounds. They're wonderful to munch while you're cooking, or to keep your guests from getting too restless if dinner is a little delayed. They come in airtight bags and will keep indefinitely at room temperature.

What to Buy Absolutely Fresh

For the best outcome of your culinary efforts, try to shop for your fresh ingredients the day before you plan to cook, or even on the same day if time allows, especially for the fish if you plan to serve it raw. It's even a good idea to check with the proprietor of your local fish market or your supermarket butcher a few days ahead to request that he set aside his best cuts for you, and always ask for *sushi*-grade fish. Avoid frozen ingredients, and use them only if you can't find fresh, and only if you plan to cook them.

Leafy vegetables can become limp and dehydrated in the refrigerator overnight if not stored properly, and although *tofu* keeps for weeks in its original sealed package, it goes bad very quickly once it has been opened.

Remember, buy only the freshest and the best, and serve it as soon as possible. ✾

Wasa

Where to Shop for Ingredients

Sushi-grade fish and shellfish for home consumption should only be purchased from a trusted local fish merchant, where you can speak personally with the proprietor about the quality and safety of the fish. If you plan to serve it raw, do not buy pre-packaged fish at a grocery chain.

Pre-packaged fish on display at the supermarket, no matter how fresh and tempting it may look, is not typically 'sushi grade' and may therefore be unsafe to eat raw.

If you find that your city or town lacks a fish market that carries *sushi*-grade seafoods, it is possible to order a nice selection online with overnight shipping at Catalina Offshore Products. **www.catalinaoop.com**

Fresh vegetables such as cucumbers, carrots, and avocados are available in any neighborhood grocery store. However, esoteric items such as *daikon*, *shiso* leaf, and *shitake* mushrooms may be harder to find and may require a trip to a gourmet grocer or an Asian market.

For commercially packaged ingredients such as *tofu*, *miso*, rice wine vinegar, *nori*, *wasabi* powder, and pickled ginger, if you live in a large metropolitan area, you should have no problem locating an Asian grocer, if not several of them, one or more of which may specialize exclusively in Japanese foods. If you live in the suburbs or in a rural area, your quest may be a little more difficult. You might have to drive into the city to find the things you need, although many upscale grocery stores and gourmet food shops in smaller towns often carry a limited inventory of Japanese ingredients. If your city has a Cost Plus World Market or Trader Joe's, you may be able to find Japanese ingredients there.

If there is a *sushi* bar in your town, you might consider asking the proprietor to give you the names of his suppliers, or even to sell you small quantities of his bulk ingredients. Of course, buying local is always your best bet, since you can examine the quality of the ingredients and compare products. But in a pinch, it's also possible to order the basics online at one of the following websites:

SushiFoods.com
A nice selection of both basic and exotic *sushi* ingredients.

AsianFoodGrocer.com
This site offers quite a wide selection of hard-to-find Japanese ingredients at reasonable prices.

EthnicGrocer.com
Offers a reasonably good selection of Japanese ingredients at fair market prices, but with several conspicuous omissions.

Wasabi

Nutritional Value

Fish and shellfish are rich in protein, vitamins, and minerals, as well as taurine, an amino acid instrumental in the digestion of fats. While some fish, especially tuna and salmon, are high in fat, the Omega-3 fatty acids found in fish are actually beneficial to health. Seaweeds such as *nori*, *wakame* and *kombu* are rich in Vitamin A, calcium, phosphorous and fiber.

Listed below are the most common types of *sushi* fish and their caloric values, based upon a single piece of *nigiri sushi* that includes 20 g. (.7 oz.) of rice at about 30 calories, with 1 g. (.04 oz.) of protein and 16 g. (.6 oz.) of carbohydrates. So, with the exception of large or fatty items such as *futomaki*, *inarizushi*, or *toro*, a pair of *nigiri sushi* averages anywhere from 70 to 120 calories, with about 32 g. (1.1 oz.) of carbohydrates.

Aji	Horse mackerel	52 calories
Akagai	Red clam	39 calories
Amaebi	Sweet shrimp	35 calories
Anago	Conger eel	61 calories
Aoyagi	Surf clam	42 calories
Awabi	Abalone	36 calories
Battera	Mackerel (Pressed-*sushi*)	93 calories
Buri	Yellowtail	60 calories
Futomaki	Thick roll (1/4 roll)	109 calories

Hamachi	Young yellowtail	59 calories
Hirame	Flounder	39 calories
Hamaguri	Clam	40 calories
Hotategai	Giant scallop	45 calories
Ika	Squid	39 calories
Ikura	Salmon roe	53 calories
Inari-zushi	Bean curd pouch	93 calories
Iwashi	Sardine	63 calories
Kaki	Oyster	40 calories
Kani	Crab	44.9 calories
Kanpyou maki	*Kanpyo* roll (1/3 roll / 2 pcs)	55 calories
Kappa maki	Cucumber roll (1/3 roll /2 pcs)	34 calories
Katsuo	Bonito	46 calories
Kazunoko	Herring roe	42 calories
Kisu	Whiting	40 calories
Kobashira	Surf clam adductors	41 calories
Kohada	Gizzard shad	52 calories
Kurumaebi	Prawn (Steamed)	45 calories
Kurumaebi	Prawn (Raw)	41 calories
Maguro (Akami)	Tuna (Non-fatty)	45 calories
Maguro (Chuutoro)	Tuna (Semi-fatty)	57 calories
Maguro (Ootoro)	Tuna (Fatty)	70 calories
Mirugai	Geoduck	38 calories
Saba	Mackerel	59 calories
Sake	Salmon	60 calories

Sayori	Halfbeak	45 calories
Shako	Mantis shrimp	47 calories
Shirauo	Whitefish	37 calories
Suzuki	Sea bass	39 calories
Tai	Red sea bream, Red snapper	43 calories
Tairagai	Pen shell	36 calories
Tako	Octopus	37 calories
Tamago	Omelet	60 calories
Tarako	Cod roe	40 calories
Tekka maki	Tuna roll (1/3 roll / 2 pcs)	49 calories
Torigai	Cockle	45 calories
Uni	Sea urchin	43 calories

Health and Safety Concerns

When it comes to *sushi*, the two main health and safety concerns are parasites and proper handling. Freshwater fish are most susceptible to parasites, mainly sea lice, worms, and the eggs they leave behind as they burrow through the flesh. Among ocean-going fish, tuna and salmon are particularly suspect, especially in warm weather. Salmon traverse the coastal waters between salty and fresh for their annual trip upstream to spawn, and the time the fish spend in fresh water can leave them infested with harmful parasites. Commercially cultivated Atlantic salmon have a much lower likelihood of common parasites, and are therefore the safest to use for *sushi*. To prepare wild salmon for safe consumption as *sushi*, the meat must undergo one or more purification techniques, including freezing at 32°F (0°C) for 72 hours, curing with salt, marinating in rice vinegar, or smoking. When properly cultivated and prepared, raw salmon is safe for *sushi*.

An experienced *sushi* chef knows how to spot the telltale signs of parasitic infestation and will take precautions against buying or serving tainted fish. Fish labeled 'sushi grade' means that it is extremely high in quality, has been shipped and handled properly, has been kept separate from other types of fish, is free of parasites, and is therefore safe to eat raw.

Ama ebi, sweet shrimp served raw as *sushi*, come from the cold, deep Northern waters on the periphery of the Arctic Circle, where there is little or no danger of parasites, and therefore *ama ebi* are safe to eat raw. All other varieties of shrimp are served cooked.

Proper handling of fish is more complex and involves how it has been stored, packaged, shipped, and if frozen, how it was thawed, not to mention the hygiene of those with whom it came into contact, including fishermen, dock workers, fish merchants, kitchen staff, and the *itamae-san* who turns it into *sushi*.

Wasabi, ginger, rice vinegar, green tea and *sake* are all believed to be bacterial combatants. However, consuming these accompaniments with *sushi* is no guarantee of protection. The Japanese term for food poisoning is *shoku-chudoku*, and the most effective way of avoiding *sushi*-related illness is to frequent only establishments with the highest standards of quality and an experienced, trustworthy staff. 🦐

World Record *Sushi*

The Longest Sushi roll to date was a *kappa maki* cucumber roll, 1,335.25 m. long (4,381 ft.), weighing over 1,200 kg. (about 2,640 lbs.) in Ichinoseki City, Japan on October 8, 2001, where it took 2,600 people an hour and a half to roll.

The longest *kaitenzushi* conveyor belt is at *Sakae Sushi* in Singapore, at 129 m. (423 ft.). Following a distant second is at Yo! Sushi in London, at 60 m. (197 ft.).

The oldest *sushi* shop is at Sushiman in Osaka, Japan, established in 1653. The oldest *sushi* shop in Tokyo is Ginza Sushi-Ei, established in 1848. Established in 1958, the oldest kaitenzushi shop is Mawaru Genroku-zushi in Higashi-osaka City in Osaka, Japan, which featured the first rolling conveyor belt.

The most expensive fish in *sushi* history was a 202 kg. (445 lbs.) bluefin tuna that sold for 20,200,000 yen ($173,853 at 116 yen to the U.S. dollar) on January 5, 2001 at Tokyo's Tsukiji Fish Market. 🐟

Sushi Merchandise

The international love affair with *sushi* has spawned a multitude of *sushi*-inspired merchandise, including lollipops molded and decorated to look exactly like the real thing, refrigerator magnets, candles, soap, erasers, keychains, jewelry, clocks, wind-up toys, posters, stationery, playing cards, comic books, fabric with *sushi* motifs for aprons and pajamas, and t-shirts featuring clever *sushi* puns. Many such items are available at Asian markets and gift shops, as well as from online merchants. A simple keyword search using '*sushi* candy', '*sushi* magnet', '*sushi* t-shirt,' etc. will yield dozens of results from which to choose. 🍥

Books About *Sushi*

Asian Tapas and Wild Sushi:
A Nibblers Delight of Fusion Cooking
by Trevor Hooper, Nancy Cooperman Su (Editor)

D.K.'s Sushi Chronicles from Hawaii:
Recipes from Sansei Seafood Restaurant & Sushi Bar
by Bonnie Friedman

Easy Sushi by Emi Kazuko
by Peter Cassidy

Easy Sushi Rolls and Miso Soups
by Fiona Smith, Diana Miller

Encyclopedia of Sushi Rolls
by Ken Kawasumi, Laura Driussi (Translator)

First Book of Sushi (World Snacks)
by Amy Wilson Sanger

Fun & Fancy Sushi
by Seiko Ogawa, Ine Mizuno

Hana Sushi: Colorful & Fun Sushi for Parties
by Boutique Sha

Inspector Morimoto and the Sushi Chef:
A Detective Story set in Japan
by Timothy Hemion

Japanese Vegetarian Cooking:
From Simple Soups to Sushi (Vegetarian Cooking Series)
by Patricia Richfield

Quick & Easy Sushi Cook Book
by Heihachiro Toyama, et al

Quick and Easy Sushi Cookbook
by Heihachiro Tohyama, Yukiko Moriyama

Roll & Sushi from Technic to Art
by Nam Chun Wha, Gang Dae Soo

Squeamish About Sushi:
And Other Foods Adventures in Japan
by Betty Reynolds

Sushi (Essential Kitchen Series)
by Ryuichi Yoshii
Sushi (Quick & Easy)
by Andreas Furtmayr

Sushi American Style
by Tracy Griffith

Sushi and Sashimi: Simple Food, Fresh Flavours
by Yasuko Fukuoka

Sushi at Home
by Kay Shimizu

Sushi
by Lulu Grimes

Sushi
by Mia Detrick

Sushi for Beginners
by Marian Keyes

Sushi for Dummies
by Judi Strada, Mineko Takane Moreno

*Sushi for Kids: Children's Introduction
to Japan's Favorite Food*
by Kaoru Ono, et al

Sushi for Parties: Maki-Zushi and Nigiri-Zushi
by Ken Kowasumi

Sushi for Wimps: Seaweed to Dragon Rolls for the Faint of Heart
by Aya Imatani, Matt Cohen (Photographer)
Sushi Made Easy
by Kumfoo

Sushi Made Easy
by Nobuko Tsuda

Sushi Modern (Essential Kitchen Series)
by Hideo Dekura

Sushi Secrets
by Kazuko Masui, Chihiro Masui

Sushi: 55 Authentic and Innovative Recipes for Nigiri, Nori-Maki, Chirashi and More!
by Yasuko Fukuoka

Sushi: A Pocket Guide
by Minori Fukuda, Kit Shan Li

Sushi: Making at Home
by Yasuko Kamimura, Kazuhiko Nagai

Sushi: Taste and Techniques
by Kimiko Barber, et al

The Best 50 Sushi Rolls (Best 50 Series)
by Carol M. Newman

The Book of Sushi
by Kinjiro Omae, Yuzuru Tachibana

The Complete Book Of Sushi
by Hideo Dekura, et al

***The Connoisseur's Guide to Sushi: Everything You Need to
Know About Sushi Varieties and Accompaniments, Etiquette
and Dining Tips and More***
by Dave Lowry

The Great Sushi and Sashimi Cookbook
by Masakazu Hori

The Little Black Book Of Sushi
by Day Zschock, Kerren Barbas (Illustrator)

***The Seafood Cookbook: 200 Recipes For Sushi, Shellfish,
Mollusks & Fish***
by Richard Carroll (Compiler)

***The Sushi Cookbook: A Step-By-Step Guide to This Popular
Japanese Food***
by Katsuji Yamamoto, Roger Hicks

Vegetarian Sushi (Essential Kitchen)
by Brigid Treloar

Vegetarian Sushi Made Easy
by Hiroko Fukuhara

A Pronunciation Guide and *Sushi* Glossary

Pronunciation Guide

The spoken Japanese language consists of a syllabary, in which each consonant sound has a vowel attached to it. The basic consonants are *a-i-u-e-o* (pronounced '*ah*', '*ee*', '*ooh*', '*eh*', '*oh*.' Each syllable and each single vowel is pronounced, and vowels and consonants are always pronounced the same way.

Vowel sounds:

a – as in father
i – as in ski
u – as in tube
e – as in hey
o – as in own

Consonant sounds:

k – as in kiss
g – as in give
s – as in summer
sh – as in shop
z – as in zoo
j – as in jump

t – as in time
ts – as in gets
ch – as in charm
n – as in new
h – as in home
b – as in baby
p – as in pet
m – as in man
ya – as in yacht
w – as in wish

f – a subtle combination of f and wh. To pronounce the syllable '*fu*,' form the '*f*' with the lips, but pronounce '*wh*' as in
'*who*.' It's more of a small puff of air than an actual syllable.

r – a subtle combination of r and d. To pronounce the syllable
'*ra*' , form the '*r*' with the lips and tongue, but pronounce '*da*.'
It takes awhile, but practice makes perfect.

There are also a few more complex combination syllables,
such as '*kyu*', '*byo*,' and '*mya*.' They are pronounced much like
English contractions, *k'yu*, *b'yo* and *m'ya*.

Long vowels are usually indicated in English with a diacritical
mark, and are pronounced as two identical syllables. The
Japanese word for no is '*iie*,' and is pronounced '*ee-a*.'

All syllables receive the same amount of stress or emphasis, so
there are no up and down inflections. For example, *maguro* is
pronounced *ma-gu-ro*, not *ma-GU-ro*.

Glossary

Aburage – Thin slices of deep-fried *tofu*, used to make *inarizushi*.

Aburana – The rape plant, used mostly for its oil, but its greens are also served as a vegetable.

Aemono – A mixture of cooked vegetables with a dressing or sauce.

Agari – A Japanese *sushi*-bar term for freshly drawn green tea, a shortened form of *agaribana*, which means 'above all.'

Agedashi – Deep-fried foods served with soy sauce, grated ginger and shredded *daikon*.

Agedofu – Deep-fried *tofu*

Agemono – Deep-fried foods such as *tempura*.

Ainame – A freshwater rock trout or greenling, sometimes served as *sashimi*.

Aji – A horse mackerel or jack fish, often served as *sashimi*.

Aji no tataki – Spanish mackerel *sashimi*, sliced from a small mackerel and served in the hollowed-out remains of its own carcass.

Ajinomoto – A popular brand of MSG (monosodium glutamate).

Ajishio – Seasoned salt, usually with MSG.

Ajitsuke – A seasoning or flavoring agent.

Ajitsuke nori – Seasoned *nori*.

Akadashi – *Miso* soup made with *akamiso*, a reddish soybean paste.

Akagai – A red clam, a burrowing mollusk, also called *peponita*, cockle or ark shell, with tender, rosy flesh. Often eaten raw.

Akajiso – Red perilla, the leaves of the beefsteak plant, sometimes used as a coloring agent, especially for *umeboshi* (sour pickled plums).

Akami – A cut of lean, red tuna from the upper and inner side of the fish near the spine.

Akodai – A red rockfish with silvery skin and horizontal stripes, native to the rocky northern coastlines of Europe and North America.

Amadai – A tilefish native to western Japan.

Amaebi – A sweet translucent shrimp, native to cold northern waters, usually served raw with its head and tentacles served deep-fried.

Amazake – A hot beverage made from water, cooked rice and a thick fermenting starter called *koji*, sweetened and seasoned with ginger. A popular New Year beverage, and as a medicinal toddy for colds and sore throats.

Ami – A tiny variety of shrimp, often made into pickled appetizers such as *shiokara*.

Anago – A conger eel, a dark, snake-like ocean fish native to tropical coastal waters, always served cooked.

Anakyu – *Makizushi* rolls filled with saltwater eel (*anago*).

Ankimo – Monkfish liver, steamed or sautéed and dressed with vinegar.

Anko – A monkfish, native to the north Atlantic, also known as an anglerfish for the tendrils it uses for luring prey.

Aojiso – A *shiso* leaf, a perilla, also known as the beefsteak plant, a member of the mint family. Used as a garnish for *sushi* and *sashimi*, and also fried *tempura*-style.

Aonori – Green laver, toasted seaweed flakes sprinkled on various foods as a condiment or seasoning.

Aoriika – A mantled squid, a ten-tentacled cephalopod with triangular fins.

Aoyagi – A surf clam or round clam, often eaten raw but turns brilliant red when steamed.

Ara – A sawedged perch with spiny fins, a freshwater fish native to Europe and North America.

Arame – A mild brown ocean algae, most commonly cooked with root vegetables as a side dish.

Arai – A style of *sashimi* preparation in which the fish is immersed in ice water to freshen its flavor before serving.

Asakusanori – Purple laver, the most common variety of algae, used to make sheets of toasted seaweed paper.

Asari – A short-necked clam, always served cooked, sometimes in vinegared appetizers called *sunomono*.

Asatsuki – Chives, often served as a garnish for *fugu sashimi*.

Aspergillus – A type of mold used to make *koji*, a starter for many fermented foods.

Awabi – An abalone, a large gastropod with a nacreous shell, native to the north Pacific, a rare seasonal delicacy, especially for *sashimi*. Often commercially cultivated.

Awasemiso – A blended *miso*, highly favored for making *miso* soup.

Ayu – A small, sweet freshwater fish, native to the rivers of Japan, caught using trained cormorant birds. Usually served grilled.

Azuki – Small, dark red beans used in a variety of Japanese dishes and pastries.

Bai – A small sea snail, or whelk, used for making vinegared *sunomono* appetizers.

Bancha – Common Japanese green tea.

Barazushi – A bowl of vinegared rice topped with slices of raw fish and other *sushi* ingredients. Also called *chirashizushi* (scattered *sushi*), or *gomokuzushi* (five-item *sushi*).

Baran – Aspidistra, an edible evergreen plant with large leaves, often grown as a houseplant.

Basashi – *Sashimi* of horsemeat, served with garlic and ginger-infused soy sauce. Especially popular in Kumamoto and Nagano.

Bateira – A turban shell, a conical shellfish, often served as a vingared *sunomono* appetizer.

Battera – Osaka-style box *sushi*, with a layer of pressed rice topped with pickled mackerel and a paper-thin slice of *konbu* sea kelp. Also called *oshizushi*.

Benishoga – Red pickled ginger, colored with sour plum vinegar and red *shiso* leaf.

Benitade – A water pepper with spicy purple leaves, sometimes served as an accompaniment for *sashimi*.

Benizake – A small sockeye salmon native to rivers and tributaries of the north Pacific.

Bento – A boxed meal of rice, pickles, and certain types of *sushi*, often taken to school or work, and widely sold to travelers as *ekiben* in railway stations. *Makunouchi* is a common style, while *shokado* is formal and elegant.

Bera – A rainbowfish, native to the fresh waters of South America and the West Indies, commonly used to make *kamaboko* fish paste.

Bettarazuke – *Daikon* radish pickled with *koji* fermenting starter.

Beruga – The Japanese pronunciation of Beluga caviar, sturgeon eggs.

Biru – The Japanese pronunciation of beer.

Bincho maguro – An albacore, also called *shiro maguro* (white tuna), with light pink flesh, often served seared on the outside.

Bora – A gray mullet with a cylindrical body and a pair of feeders on its chin, native to warm coastal waters around the world. Sometimes served as *sashimi*.

Botan ebi – A botan shrimp, sweet and translucent, sometimes served with its own blue roe.

Budai – A parrotfish, a colorful tropical fish with a beak-like tooth formation.

Buri – A yellowtail or amberjack, a mature type of *hamachi*, often served as *sashimi* or *nigiri sushi*, especially popular at New Year celebrations.

California roll* – *Makizushi* rolls filled with crab, avocado and cucumber. By far the most popular specialty *makizushi* rolls in the U.S., their invention is attributed to Itamae-san Mashita of Tokyo Kaikan Restaurant of Los Angeles, which is no longer in operation. The California roll has undergone many evolutions since its invention in the early 1970s, most are now made with the rice on the outside, and garnished with sesame seeds or flying fish roe.

Calpis – A sweet soft drink derived from milk, similar in taste to barley water.

Caterpillar roll* – *Makizushi* rolls with thin slices of raw fish and avocado wrapped around the outside of a California roll. Another name for Rainbow roll, *Geisha* roll, or Dragon roll.

Cha – The Japanese word for tea, available in many types and grades of quality. Also called *ocha*.

Chakin-zushi – *Sushi* rice wrapped in a thin egg omelet.

Chawan mushi – A savory steamed egg custard served in a *chawan* tea mug.

Chinmi – A Japanese term used to describe a rare delicacy, the three most prized being *uni*, *konowata* and *karasumi*.

Chirashizushi – A bowl of vinegared rice with slices of raw fish and other *sushi* toppings. Its name means 'scattered *sushi*,' also known as *barazushi*, or *gomokuzushi* (five-item *sushi*).

Chomiryo – The Japanese word for 'seasoning' or 'condiment.'

Chosame – A sturgeon, native to northern waters, especially valued for its caviar, but its flesh is never eaten raw. Its Japanese name means 'butterfly shark.'

Chu-toro – The semi-fatty cut of *maguro*, taken from the lower broad side of the tuna.

Chutoro maki – *Makizushi* rolls filled with semi-fatty tuna.

Daidai – A bitter Japanese citrus fruit, also called Seville orange. Its juice is mixed with soy sauce to make *ponzu*.

Daidai su – Bitter orange vinegar flavored with Seville orange.

Daikon – A large, carrot-shaped white radish (*Raphanus sativus*), commonly used in Japanese cuisine. A *daikon* can weigh up to seven pounds and is often served pickled, or finely shredded as an attractive garnish for some Japanese dishes, especially *sashimi*.

Daikon-oroshi – Finely shredded *daikon* radish, usually served as a garnish for *sashimi* and other *sushi*.

Dashi – An all-purpose stock for soups and simmered dishes usually made with *kombu* (a type of seaweed) and flavored with dried *shiitake* or *katsuoboshi* (bonito flakes).

Datemaki – A sweet rolled omelet made with eggs and white-fish, especially popular at New Year celebrations.

Datsu – A Pacific needlefish, also called a sea pike, a predatory fish with a cylindrical body and elongated jaw, native to northern coastal waters. Commonly used to make *kamaboko* fish paste.

Denbu – Dried whitefish and shrimp paste, colored red and shredded, most commonly used in *futomaki* or as a topping for *chirashizushi*.

Doburoku – Home-brewed *sake*. Thick, actively fermenting, and illegal.

Dragon roll* – *Makizushi* roll with thin slices of raw fish and avocado wrapped around the outside of a California roll. Another name for Rainbow roll, *Geisha* roll, or Caterpillar roll.

Dynamite roll* – *Makizushi* roll filled with spicy tuna, salmon, *hamachi*, etc.

Ebi – A shrimp, any of a wide variety of species. Usually refers to the cooked variety served as *nigiri sushi*.

Ebi no atama – Shrimp heads, served deep-fried as a side dish with an order of *amaebi*, raw sweet shrimp.

Ebi Tempura maki – *Makizushi* rolls filled with *tempura* shrimp.

Edamame – A type of young green soybean, boiled in the pods. This summer treat is a popular *sushi* bar appetizer, or a complimentary snack food served alongside cold draft beers in Japanese *izakaya* pubs, where patrons pop open the pods much like salted peanuts, and munch on the tasty beans within. Also called *sayamame*.

Edomaezushi – Tokyo-style *nigiri sushi*. Its name means 'in front of Tokyo.'

Engawa – The small muscle around the fin of a flounder or halibut, or the meat surrounding the muscle in a scallop, a delicacy usually eaten raw.

Enoki-take – A tiny white mushroom that grows in bunches during the winter months.

Fugu – A blowfish, globefish or pufferfish, with a spiny body that can inflate with air or water when threatened. Although a deadly toxin is contained in its liver and ovaries, it is nevertheless popular as an edible delicacy when properly prepared.

Fuka – A large carnivorous shark with tough skin and rugged scales.

Fuki – A butterbur plant, similar to rhubarb or celery, commonly used for pickles.

Fukijinzuke – A popular Japanese pickle medley, usually composed of seven vegetables, including *daikon*, eggplant, lotus root, ginger, *shiso* buds, turnip, *shitake* mushrooms, and other vegetables native to Japan.

Fukko – A young freshwater perch with spiny fins.

Fukusa-zushi – *Sushi* wrapped with thin omelet.

Funa – A crucian carp, a lake-dwelling goldfish, most commonly used to make *sashimi* and Osaka-style pressed *sushi*.

Funamori – Another name for *gunkanmaki*. Its name means 'boat wrap.'

Furikake – A condiment or topping blend of seaweed flakes, sesame seeds and dried fish powder.

Futomaki – Much like *maki* rolls, *futomaki* is an oversized *nori* roll, filled with a colorful assortment of rice, cucumber, red ginger, pink fish cake, dried gourd, pickled yellow radish, and egg omelet. When sliced, the colorful ingredients inside form an attractive pattern in the center of each piece.

Gari – Pickled ginger, thinly sliced and served as an accompaniment to *sushi*. Also called *garishoga*.

Gazami – A blue crab, also called *watarigani*, native to the coastal waters of Japan.

Geisha roll* – *Makizushi* roll with thin slices of raw fish and avocado wrapped around the outside of a California roll. Also called Rainbow roll, Caterpillar roll, and Dragon roll.

Genmai su – Brown rice vinegar.

Geso – Squid tentacles, often prepared with *teriyaki* sauce.

Gindara – A sablefish, native to the Bering Sea. Usually served cooked.

Ginzake – A small coho salmon, native to the Great Lakes and the coastal waters of the north Pacific.

Gizami – A rainbowfish, native to the fresh waters of South America and the West Indies, commonly used to make *kamaboko* fish paste. Also called *bera*.

Gobo – A burdock, a bitter root vegetable, often mixed with carrot in a dish called *kinpira gobo*.

Gohan – The Japanese word for plain cooked rice. Also the word for 'meal.'

Goma – Sesame seeds, widely used as a garnish for *makizushi*.

Goma shio – Sesame salt, a blend of salt and ground sesame seeds, commonly found on Japanese tables.

Gomokuzushi – A bowl of vinegared rice with slices of raw fish and other *sushi* toppings. Its name means 'five item *sushi*.' Also known as *chirashizushi* or *barazushi*.

Gunkan – Its name means 'battleship.' and *gunkan sushi* is another type of *nori* roll, in which the narrow strip of seaweed paper extends slightly beyond the top of the ball of vinegared rice, creating a shallow niche to hold a small serving of a soft ingredient such as fish roe, sea urchin, or minced shellfish.

Gunkan Maki – Battleship roll, an alternate name for *kakomi sushi*.

Gyokairui – A general term for seafood.

Gyokuro – Japan's rarest, most expensive tea, *gyokuro* is made from the tender first tea leaves of spring.

Gyoran – A general term for fish roe.

Gyosho – The Japanese name for Asian fish sauce. Also called n*uoc mam*, *patis*, and *nam pla*.

Hage – A filefish or leather fish, a flat, narrow fish with leathery skin, native to warm waters. Often served as *sashimi*.

Hajikami – A ginger shoot, often served pickled.

Hakko – A general term for fermentation.

Hakumai – Polished white rice.

Hakusai – Chinese cabbage, often used in vinegared dishes called *tsukemono*.

Hama bofu – A seaside plant, often served with *sashimi*, or as a garnish for vinegared fish *sunomono*.

Hamachi – A young yellowtail with a distinctive yellow stripe along its sides and tail, native to the tropical waters of the Atlantic and Caribbean.

Hamachi kama – Yellowtail shoulder, a small, delicate piece of fish just behind the head. Usually served grilled.

Hamaguri – A clam, usually served steamed or fried as *yaki hamaguri*, and rarely served raw.

Hamo – A conger eel or pike conger native to Japan, very bony and always served cooked. Often used for *oshizushi*, Osaka-style pressed *sushi*.

Hanami – Cherry blossom season, a time when *sushi* is especially popular as a traditional food for flower viewing parties.

Hanasakigani – A blue king crab, native to the waters surrounding the northern waters of *Hokkaido*.

Harusame – Thin, transparent mung bean gelatin noodles. Often used in *sunomono* appetizers.

Hasu – Lotus root, also known as *renkon*.

Hata – A grouper, a bottom-dweller native to tropical seas.

Hata-hata – A sailfin or sandfish, two types of small silver scaleless burrowing fish, native to the north Pacific.

Haze – A goby, a fish native to many waters including Tokyo Bay. Often served as *sashimi*.

Hechima – A loofa gourd, sometimes served in vinegared *sunomono* appetizers.

Hichimi Togarashi – A mixture of seven spices, including red pepper (*togarashi*), ground *sansho*, pepper pods, dried mandarin orange peel, hemp seeds, poppy seeds, *nori* seaweed flakes, and sesame seeds.

Hijiki – A dark, brown seaweed that turns black when dried.

Hikarimono – A general term for any variety of silver fish, its name literally means 'shiny things.' Also, fish sliced for serving with the silver skin left intact, especially *aji*, *sanma*, and *kohada*.

Himo – The fringe or mantle of an ark shell.

Hiramasa – A gold-striped amberjack native to warm seas.

Hirame – A flounder or halibut, a flat fish with delicate flesh and a migrating eye, native to the waters of North America and Europe.

Hirame Usuzukuri – A method of preparing halibut *sashimi* in very thin, translucent slices, served with *ponzu* sauce.

Hiratake – Oyster mushroom.

Hishio – A category of Japanese pickled and fermented dishes that includes *tsukemono* and *shiokara*.

Hiyayako – A block of cold *tofu* topped with grated ginger and spring onion.

Hobo – A bluefin tuna, the largest variety reaches 1,500 lbs. (680 kg.), migrates between tropical and polar seas.

Hokkai ebi – A shrimp native to the waters around the northern island of Hokkaido.

Hokke – A greenling or mackerel, native to the northern Pacific, usually served grilled.

Hokki gai – A red-tipped surf clam, also called hen clam, off-white when served as *sashimi* and *sushi*, but turns bright pink when cooked.

Horagai – A conch, a spiral-shelled gastropod, native to warm tropical waters, with firm, mildly flavored white flesh, served as *sashimi* and *sushi*, and also in vinegared *sunomono* appetizers.

Horenso – Spinach, which is used in many Japanese dishes.

Hoshi garei – A spotted plaice, a large European flatfish.

Hotaru ika – A firefly squid.

Hotategai – A giant sea scallop, a fan-shaped mollusk with, mild, sweet, delicate white flesh. Its roe is also considered a delicacy.

Hotategai kaibashira – The adductor muscle of a sea scallop, considered a delicacy.

Hoya – A sea squirt, a tiny, sedentary invertebrate with a sac-like body with siphons that can contract to eject streams of water to escape predators. Their flesh is eaten raw, and their intestines are mixed with vinegar to make *sunomono*, or fermented to make *shiokara*.

Ibodai – A butterfish, a slippery, scaleless fish native to North Atlantic coastal waters.

Igai – A mussel, a freshwater bivalve mollusk, usually served steamed.

Iidako – A baby octopus, usually served boiled and marinated in a sweet soy sauce.

Ika – A squid, a cuttlefish, a tubular translucent, tentacled cephalopod, usually served thinly sliced with *shiso* leaf.

Ika sansai – Marinated squid with mountain vegetables.

Ika somen – Squid 'noodles,' thinly sliced raw squid mixed with quail egg, *wasabi*, and seaweed.

Ika mentai – Squid with spicy *mentaiko* cod roe, served as *sashimi* or used to fill *makizushi* or *temaki* hand rolls.

Ika natto – Thinly sliced squid mixed with fermented soybeans. Sometimes used as a filling for *makizushi* or *temaki*.

Ika no sengiri – Very thinly sliced squid, its name means 'a thousand slices.'

Ika no shiokara – Fermented squid entrails, salty and pale pink in color.

Ika-geso – Squid tentacles, often prepared with *teriyaki* sauce.

Ikkyu – A premium grade rice wine.

Ikura – Salmon roe, large, bright orange fish eggs filled with salty juice, often served as *gunkan-maki* or as a delicate garnish on other types of *sushi*.

Imo – A Japanese word for potato, including yams, sweet potatoes, and taro root.

Inada – A very young yellowtail.

Inarizushi – Pouches of deep-fried *tofu* filled with vinegared rice and other ingredients, such as pickles and sour plums.

Irigoma – Toasted sesame seeds.

Inryo – A general term for Japanese beverages.

Isaki – A grunt fish, native to tropical seas, named for the grunting sound it makes. Often served as *sashimi*.

Ise ebi – A spiny lobster, a saltwater crustacean, usually served grilled at New Year celebrations.

Ishidai – A parrotfish, a colorful tropical fish with a beak-like tooth formation.

Ishigakidai – A rock porgy, a lean fish native to tropical coastal waters worldwide.

Isobe – A general term for anything wrapped in or garnished with *nori*.

Itawasa – *Kamaboko* fish paste, sliced and served with *wasabi* and soy sauce.

Itayagi – A small bay scallop, native to coastal Japan and other parts of the world.

Iwana – A char, any of several small-scaled trout, native to cold streams.

Iwashi – A sardine or herring, small fish that swims in large schools, native to the coastal waters in many parts of the world. Sometimes served as *sashimi* or grilled. Usually available canned.

Izumidai – A tilapia fish, similar in appearance to snapper or *tai*, with firm translucent flesh and red stripes.

Ji mono – A general term for items of local specialty, including fish, pickles, *sake*, etc.

Kabocha – A pumpkin or winter squash, widely used in a variety of dishes including *tempura*.

Kabu – A Japanese turnip, widely used in pickles as well as other dishes.

Kai – A general term for any kind of mollusk, such as oysters, mussels, clams, etc.

Kaibashira – The adductor muscle of a shellfish, such as scallop, or clam, often served as *sashimi*, *sushi*, or *sunomono*.

Kaiso – A general term for seaweed.

kaiware – *Daikon* sprouts, peppery young shoots used as garnish or salad.

Kaiware maki – *Makizushi* rolls filled with peppery *daikon* radish sprouts.

Kajika – A bullhead catfish, a freshwater fish with a large head and long whiskers.

Kajiki – A swordfish, a large, toothless fish with a long sword-like snout, native to the ocean floor of warm waters. Often eaten as *sashimi* or *sushi*.

Kaki – An oyster, a mollusk with a rough nacreous shell, native to coastal waters all over the world, served on the half-shell in sushi bars, and also popular fried.

Kakomi sushi – Another name for *gunkan maki* or *funamori*.

Kamaboko – A fish paste made with mild white fish, and molded into various shapes, most commonly imitation crab.

Kamasu – A barracuda, a carnivorous marine fish with a cylindrical body and large mouth with a protruding lower jaw and long teeth.

Kan – A counting unit for *nigiri sushi*, one piece.

Kani – A crab, any of several varieties, always served cooked, and often substituted with imitation crab made from whitefish paste.

Kani miso – The brown entrails inside a boiled crab shell, valued as a delicacy in Japan, straight from the shell or prepared in a sauce of rice wine, sugar and egg.

Kanpachi – An amberjack, also spelled *kampachi*, several types of copper-colored fish, native to warm tropical waters.

Kanpyo – Dried strips of the *yugao* gourd, also known as calabash, a tropical American evergreen that produces large bottle-shaped gourds, used in many Japanese dishes.

Kanpyo maki – *Makizushi* rolls filled with pickled *kanpyo* gourd.

Kappa – A *sushi* term for fresh cucumber, named for the *kappa*, a mythical water genie from Japanese folklore who is said to be fond of cucumbers.

Kappa maki – *Makizushi* filled with strips of fresh cucumber.

Karafuto masu – A type of pink salmon, especially valued for its roe.

Karashi – A hot Japanese mustard made from the seeds of several varieties of mustard plants.

Karashi sumiso – White *miso* seasoned with vinegar and *karashi* mustard, often served with *konnyaku*.

Karasumi – Gray mullet roe served dried and salted. One of Japan's three most prized delicacies.

Karei – A halibut, plaice, flounder, or sand dab, a flatfish with a migrating eye, native to northern waters. Especially favored for *sashimi*.

Kasago – A marbled rockfish, a spawning fish with dark horizontal stripes, native to the rocky coastal waters of Europe and North America.

Kasu – The lees or dregs of the *sake* fermentation process, sometimes used in soups and pickles.

Kasugo – A young sea bream.

Katadofu – A firm, coarse textured *tofu*.

Katakuchi-iwashi – An anchovy, a tiny Mediterranean or tropical fish, best eaten raw with ginger and soy sauce, usually available canned or salted.

Katsuo – A skipjack or *bonito*, an ocean-going variety of smaller tuna, native to both Atlantic and Pacific waters

Katsuo bushi – Blocks of dried, smoked and cured bonito, which look like pieces of driftwood. When shaved into paper-thin flakes, *katsuo* may be used as a garnish, a flavoring agent and most importantly as a base for *dashi*, the most common Japanese soup stock.

Katsuo no tataki – Dark, young tuna *sashimi*, richly flavored, aged and seared, served with ginger and green onion.

Kawahagi – A filefish or leather fish, a flat, narrow fish with leathery skin, native to warm waters.

Kawamasu – A brook trout or char, originally from North America and introduced to Japan. Usually served cooked.

Kazunoko – Herring roe, tiny, salty, bright yellow, compact herring eggs, often served at New Year celebrations.

Kegani – A horsehair crab.

Keshinomi – Delicate dried smoked bonito shavings used for garnish, flavoring, and as a base for *dashi* soup stock.

Kibinago – A banded blue sprat, a small sardine-like fish native to European waters. Usually available smoked or canned.

Kihada – A yellowfin tuna, up to 400 lbs. (181 kg.), native to tropical waters, served as *sashimi* and *sushi*.

Kikurage – A dried cloud ear mushroom, served in *sunomono* appetizers and other vegetable dishes.

Kimachi – A small fish in the yellowtail family.

Kinome – Young leaves of the *sansho* tree, a prickly ash.

Kinpira gobo – A dish of burdock root and carrot marinated in rice wine sweetened with *mirin* and sugar, and seasoned with chili pepper and soy sauce.

Kinome – Leaves of the Japanese prickly ash (*sansho*), used in soups and to flavor simmered foods.

Kisu – A silver whiting, a cod-like fish served in many different ways.

Kobashira – A surf clam.

Kobe gyutataki – *Kobe* beef lightly seared on the outside and still raw inside. A cool weather delicacy.

Kochi – A flatfish, any of several varieties with a migrating eye and a flattened body, served as *sashimi* and *sushi*.

Kohada – A Tokyo name for a gizzard shad, a herring-like spawning fish native to northern waters.

Koi – A Japanese carp, a lean, bony freshwater fish, often kept as decorative specimens in garden ponds.

Koji – A fermentation starter. Grains or beans inoculated with Aspergillus mold and used as a starter for fermented foods such as *miso, tamari, shoyu, amazake, mirin* and rice vinegar.

Komai – A yellow cod, a lean white fish native to the north Atlantic.

Kome – A Japanese term for uncooked rice.

Kona wasabi – Powdered *wasabi* root.

Konbu – A large, thick, wide sea kelp native to the waters of northern Japan, sold in dried form. Most commonly used in making *dashi*, the most common soup stock, where it softens and expands to several times its size.

Konnyaku – The root of the devil's tongue plant, a gray, rubbery, gelatinous paste sold in blocks or strands. Used to make a variety of Japanese dishes.

Ko no mono – A general term for Japanese pickles. Also called *tsukemono*.

Konoshiro – A large gizzard shad, a herring-like spawning fish native to the north Atlantic, a popular fish for *sashimi* and *sushi*.

Konowata – Fermented sea slug entrails. One of Japan's three most prized delicacies.

Koromo – A general term for dressings and batters used to coat foods.

Koshinryo – A general term for spices, including hemp seeds, sesame seeds, mustard, poppy seeds, prickly ash seeds, ginger, chili pepper, *wasabi* and citron.

Koso – A general term for herbs, including water pepper, *shiso*, and trefoil.

Koyadofu – Freeze-dried *tofu* that becomes spongy and soft when reconstituted. Sometimes used as a filler for *makizushi*.

Kujira – Whale meat, illegal in the U.S. but a popular delicacy in Japan.

Kukicha – A tea made from roasted tea twigs and stems.

Kurage – A jellyfish, usually served marinated in *sunomono* appetizers.

Kuro dai – A black porgy, a meaty fish native to warm coastal waters. Not served as *sushi* or *sashimi* because of its strong fishy smell.

Kuro goma – Black sesame seeds, used as a garnish on some kinds of *sushi*.

Kuro-su – Brown rice vinegar.

Kuruma ebi – A tiger prawn.

Kyabia – The Japanese pronunciation of caviar.

Kyuri – A Japanese cucumber, smaller than U.S. varieties and without a large seed core. Most commonly used for pickles and *sunomono* appetizers.

Ma aji – A yellow horse mackerel. The prefix '*ma*' means 'true.'

Mabikina – Tender shoots of green vegetables, often used as garnishes or as *sushi* ingredients.

Madai – A red snapper or red sea bream, any of several large sharp-toothed fish, native to tropical coastal waters.

Madai tarako-ae – Red sea bream served with cod roe.

Maguro – Any of several varieties of tuna, an ocean-going fish most popular for *sashimi* and *nigiri sushi*.

Maguro nyuta – Raw tuna mixed with *wakame* seaweed and green onion topped with *miso*.

Maguro sai-kyo yaki – Seared tuna marinated in *miso*.

Maguro temaki – *Temaki* hand roll filled with raw tuna.

Mai-take – Hen-of-the-wood, a Japanese mushroom used in many dishes.

Makajiki – A blue marlin, an ocean-going fish with a long, pointed snout.

Makizushi – This variety of *sushi* is composed of vinegared rice and bits of fish or seafood, wrapped cigar-style in a sheet of toasted seaweed paper called *nori*, and sliced into six bite-sized pieces.

Mako garei – A plaice or flatfish, native to northern waters.

Mana gatsuo – A silver pomfret, a meaty, dark-skinned fish with spiny fins, native to northern waters.

Manbo – An ocean sunfish in the perch family, with a compact, oval body, native to warm waters.

Masago – Smelt roe, tiny orange fish eggs, finer but similar in appearance to flying fish roe.

Masu – A trout, any of a variety of freshwater fish, commonly cultivated in commercial hatcheries, usually served in specialty restaurants.

Matcha – Powdered green tea used in the Japanese tea ceremony.

Mategai – A razor shell clam with a long narrow shell, named for its shape, which resembles a straight razor.

Matodai – A John Dory, a fish with a large mouth and a distinctive black spot on its side, native to Japan's southern waters.

Matsubagani – a Matsuba crab or Pacific snow crab. Also called *zuwaigani* in eastern Japan.

Matsutake – A rare and expensive wild Japanese mushroom native to Japan and other northern climates, seasonal in autumn. One of Japan's most coveted delicacies.

Mebachi maguro – An albacore, a smaller white tuna native to tropical waters, most commonly available as canned tuna, but also served as *sushi*.

Mebaru – A rock cod, a lean white fish native to the north Atlantic.

Megochi – A big-eyed flathead, a bottom-dwelling fish with a flattened snout, native to the waters of Indonesia.

Meji Maguro – A young tuna.

Mejina – A large scaled blackfish, native to coastal northern waters, and a popular choice for *sashimi*.

Mekajiki – A swordfish, a large, toothless fish with a long sword-like snout, native to the ocean floor of warm waters.

Menma – Pickled bamboo shoot.

Mentai – An Alaskan pollack or cod, rarely eaten raw, but valued for its roe.

Mentaiko – The roe of the Alaskan pollack, often mixed with cayenne pepper and colored bright red, used as a garnish for some kinds of *sushi*. Also called *karashi-mentaiko*.

Menuke – A rockfish or ocean perch, a spawning fish with dark horizontal stripes, native to the rocky coastal northern waters.

Meshi – Cooked rice. Also a Japanese word for 'meal.'

Mikan – A mandarin orange or tangerine.

Minami-maguro – A southern bluefin tuna.

Mirin – A special type of sweet rice wine used only for cooking.

Mirinboshi – Any of a variety of small fish such as *aji*, butterflied, marinated in *mirin* and soy sauce and then dried.

Mirugai – A geoduck or horse-neck clam, a very large burrowing clam with a long, muscular foot. Served sliced as *sushi*.

Mirukui – The original name for *mirugai*, a geoduck or horse-neck clam.

Miso – A fermented soybean paste, sometimes mixed with fermented barley or rice. Available in many colors and styles, used to make pickles, sauces, marinades and most importantly, *miso shiru*, a classic Japanese broth served with nearly every Japanese meal.

Miso shiru – Japan's most popular soup, a broth made with a sea kelp and dried bonito broth called *dashi*, mixed with *miso* paste and garnished with cubes of *tofu* and bits of seaweed or other vegetables.

Misozuke – Japanese pickles cured with *miso*.

Mitsuba – A trefoil plant, similar in flavor to chervil and widely used in Japanese cooking .

Mochi – Japanese rice dumplings made by pounding glutinous rice into a rubbery dough. Prepared in many ways from grilled skewers to sweet cakes.

Momendofu – A Japanese name for the common variety of *tofu*.

Momiji-oroshi – Grated *daikon* radish with red pepper.

Morijio – A small pile of salt, a Japanese purification ritual and offering to the gods for their protection. Small piles of salt can be seen at the entrances of many shrines and businesses in Japan. Salt is also placed at the entrances of bars and restaurants to attract customers.

Moritsuke – The Japanese art of food arrangement.

Moroko – A willow shiner, a small, silvery fish native to the North Atlantic and Mediterranean Sea.

Morokyu – Sliced cucumber marinated in unfiltered soy sauce.

Moromi – A Japanese term for unfiltered liquids such as *sake*, *mirin*, and soy sauce. A fermenting slurry that forms during the brewing process just before filtration.

Moromi miso – Vegetables pickled in *moromi* and *miso*, sometimes served on cucumber slices.

Motsu – A general term for entrails or giblets, used to prepare many types of Japanese dishes.

Mozuku – Delicate, dark brown seaweed often served as *sunomono* appetizers.

Mukozuke – The first course of a Japanese meal. Often used to refer to *sashimi*.

Moyashi – Bean sprouts.

Murasaki – A *sushi* bar term for soy sauce. The word means 'purple.'

Muroaji – A brown-striped mackerel native to Japan. Often served as *sashimi* or *sushi*.

Mushimono – A general term for steamed foods.

Musubi – A decorative knot or tie for certain herbs and vegetables used as a garnish for Japanese food. Also a term for rice balls filled with fish, vegetables or pickles, sometimes wrapped in *nori*. Also called *o-nigiri*.

Mutsu – A Japanese bluefish that feeds on smaller fish in shallow waters. Often served as *sashimi*.

Mutsugoro – A blue spotted goby native to the coastal waters of Japan. Usually served grilled.

Myoga – A type of ginger used for its buds and shoots rather than for its roots. Fragrant and herbaceous rather than peppery, served in salads, or pickled as a garnish for grilled fish.

Nama – A Japanese prefix that means fresh or raw. Used to describe foods and also draft beer.

Namako – A sea cucumber or sea slug, named for its cucumber-shaped body. Tough and crunchy, served raw in Japan.

Namaribushi – Partially smoked bonito, sometimes served as an appetizer with mixed vegetables.

Namasu – A dish of raw fish or meat mixed with vegetables and dressed with vinegar.

Namazu – A catfish, usually served grilled or *tempura*-style and only in specialty restaurants.

Nameko – A golden-brown Japanese mushroom, usually available pickled or in cans. Often used in soups.

Nanairo togarashi – A spice blend with seven ingredients, including red pepper (*togarashi*), ground *sansho* pepper pods, dried mandarin orange peel, black hemp seeds or white poppy seeds, *nori* seaweed bits, and white sesame seeds. Also called *shichimi togarashi*.

Nanabanzuke – Portuguese–style pickled fish.

Nanohana – The immature buds of the rape plant, similar in appearance to broccoli. Often served pickled.

Narezushi – The original form of *sushi*, a fermenting process developed in ancient Asia as a means of preserving fish.

Nashi – A Japanese pear.

Nasu – A Japanese eggplant, often used to make pickles, or as a fresh ingredient in many other dishes.

Nasu no tsukemono – Pickled eggplant.

Nasu yaki – Broiled eggplant.

Natane – The seeds of the rape plant, used for their oil. Also called canola oil.

Natto – Fermented soybeans, sticky, stinky and definitely an acquired taste. Often used as a filling for *makizushi*, or as an ingredient in many other Japanese dishes.

Natto Maki – *Makizushi* rolls filled with *natto*, sticky, stinky fermented soybeans.

Nazuke – Japanese salt pickles, made with a variety of leafy vegetables. Often served as *tsukemono*.

Negi – A scallion or spring onion, used as a simple garnish for soups and *sushi*, and in many other Japanese dishes.

Negi toro – Raw tuna mixed with green onion.

Negi-toro maki – *Makizushi* rolls filled with raw tuna and spring onion.

Nemagaritake – A Chinese bamboo shoot, used in many Japanese dishes.

Neri – A Japanese prefix which means 'prepared,' often used to describe pastes or powdered seasonings.

Neri-wasabi – Japanese horseradish paste.

Neta – A *sushi* bar term for the fish topping in *nigiri sushi*.

Niboshi – Small dried fish, especially anchovies, commonly used for making soup stocks.

Nigiri sushi – Served in pairs, this style of sushi consists of slices of raw fish or pieces of other types of seafood, placed atop oblong balls of vinegared rice. Also called *Edo-mae sushi*, which literally means 'in front of Edo,' the name of old Tokyo.

Nihaizu – A mixture of vinegar and soy sauce, sometimes diluted with *dashi*.

Nihon shu – Japanese rice wine, *sake*.

Ni ika – Squid simmered in soy sauce.

Nijimasu – A rainbow trout, a spawning fish native to the northern Pacific, widely cultivated at commercial farms in Japan. Served as *sashimi* or grilled.

Nikiri – Soy sauce that has been heated

Nikogori – A general term for congealed food.

Niku – A general term for any kind of meat.

Nikyu – A lesser grade of sake.

Ni-mono – A general term for any kind of boiled or simmered food.

Ninjin – A carrot, a term for both western varieties as well as native Japanese carrots, widely used in many Japanese dishes.

Ninniku – Garlic, widely available in Japan but used in a limited number of Japanese dishes.

Nira – Chinese chives, an important component of *gyoza* pot stickers.

Nishime – Dried foods seasoned with soy sauce, ginger and *mirin*, often included in *bento* boxes or as special New Year dishes.

Nishin – A herring, native to the northern Atlantic and Pacific, usually available salted or pickled. Also valued for its roe.

Nitsume – A general term for condensed sauces.

Nori – An edible seaweed paper made from a variety of algae called *Porphyra*, also called laver. Once it has been harvested from the sea, the algae is pulverized and laid out in thin sheets to dry. It is then cut into uniform squares and packaged for commercial distribution. *Nori* is commonly used as a wrap for *sushi* and *onigiri*, as well as a shredded topping for soups, rice and noodles.

Norimaki – *Sushi* rolled in sheets of *nori* seaweed paper with vinegared rice and various fillings.

Noritama–Egg omelet wrapped in *nori* seaweed paper.

Nozawana – Turnip greens, often used in pickles and *tsukemono*.

Nuta – A mixture of fish and vegetables dressed with *miso* and vinegar.

Oaiso – The check or bill in a *sushi* restaurant.

Oba – Perilla leaf, beefsteak plant, or *shiso*.

Oboro – Dried whitefish flakes, used as a filling for *makizushi* or as a topping for various Japanese dishes.

Oboro konbu – Dried flakes of sea kelp, used as an ingredient for *sunomono*.

Ocha – A general term for Japanese green tea.

Odori – Raw shrimp or langoustine prepared and served while still alive. Its name means 'dance.' Also called *odori ebi*.

Odorigui – Tiny whitebait fish dressed with vinegar and soy sauce and served while still alive.

Ohitashi – Par-cooked vegetables seasoned with soy sauce and *mirin*. Served chilled.

Ohyo – A Pacific halibut, a flatfish often served as *sashimi*.

Okonomizushi – Home-style *nigiri sushi*.

Okoze – A stingfish, also called stonefish or scorpion fish. A venomous tropical fish with rock-like camouflage.

Omakase – A request for the *sushi* chef to choose the *sushi* selection for the customer.

Onigiri – Balls of sticky rice, either plain or filled with various ingredients, often wrapped in *nori* seaweed paper. A popular treat for Japanese lunchboxes.

Oregon roll* – *Makizushi* roll filled with smoked salmon.

Orizume – A general term for food packed in a box lunch.

Oroshi-wasabi – Grated *wasabi* root.

Oshizushi – Osaka-style *sushi*, boxes of pressed rice topped with thin slices of fish and cut into bite-sized pieces.

Oshinko – A general term for Japanese pickles.

Oshinkomaki – *Makizushi* rolls filled with Japanese pickles, especially *daikon* radish.

Oyo – A halibut, a large flatfish with a migrating eye, native to northern waters. Often served as *sashimi*. Also called *ohyo*.

Philadelphia roll* – *Makizushi* roll filled with salmon and cream cheese.

Ponzu – A Japanese dipping sauce, soy sauce flavored with citron.

Rainbow roll* – *Makizushi* roll with thin slices of raw fish and avocado wrapped around the outside of a California roll. Also called *Geisha* roll, Caterpillar roll, and Dragon roll.

Rakkyo – Pickled scallion.

Ramune – A popular Japanese brand of bottled lemonade that comes in a distinctive blue bottle sealed with a glass marble.

Renkon – Lotus root, widely used in Japanese pickles and other dishes.

Ryori – A general term for cooking or cuisine of any kind.

Ryotei – A very high-class Japanese restaurant, with private rooms for patrons and a set menu specially designed by the chef.

Saba – A mackerel, a small, oily, red-fleshed fish with silvery skin, native to the Atlantic, available seasonally. Usually served with ginger and spring onion.

Sabazushi – Mackerel *sushi*, a general term for any kind of *sushi* made with fresh raw mackerel.

Saikyo-yaki – Fish marinated in *miso* and seared outside, leaving the inside raw.

Sakana – A general term for any kind of fish. Also a term for any kind of food that is traditionally served with *sake*.

Sake – Japanese rice wine, available in many styles and grades of quality.

Sake – A salmon, any of several varieties of spawning fish, native to cool northern waters. Susceptible to parasites in the wild, so most *sushi* grade salmon is farm raised or must be treated by freezing, salting, marinating or smoking.

Sakekawa maki – *Makizushi* rolls or *temaki* rolls filled with broiled salmon skin.

Saku – A block of fish meat.

Sakura-dai – A spring red sea bream, its name means 'cherry-blossom bream.'

Sakura ebi – A type of shrimp, its name means 'cherry blossom shrimp.'

Sakura masu – A spring salmon trout, its name means 'cherry-blossom trout.'

Sarada – The Japanese pronunciation of 'salad,' which may mean any of a number of types of fresh green dishes. Also called *nama yasai*.

Same – A shark, never served raw for *sushi*, but sometimes served marinated as *sunomono*.

Samegawa – The skin of a shark.

Sanbaizu – A mixture of vinegar, soy sauce and *mirin*, used as a dressing for seafood and vegetables.

Sanma – A mackerel pike, a freshwater fish with a long snout native to northern waters, served as *sashimi* and *sunomono* as well as in other dishes and types of preparations.

Sansai – A mixture of wild young mountain vegetables and greens indigenous to Japan. Served marinated or pickled.

Sansho – Japanese pepper, the seeds of the prickly ash, ground into a powder and used by itself or in a blend with other spices.

Sarashi negi – Thinly sliced green onion, used for *sushi* garnishes and in *ponzu* dipping sauce.

Sasa – Bamboo leaf.

Sashimi – Thin slices of raw fish, usually served with a garnish of grated *daikon* radish, *wasabi* paste, and soy sauce for dipping. Traditionally the first course of a *sushi* meal.

Sato imo – Taro root.

Sato – The Japanese word for sugar.

Satsuma-age – Deep fried fish paste, a Tokyo favorite. Also called *age-kamaboko*.

Sawagani – A river crab, tiny freshwater crabs native to Japan. Usually deep-fried and served whole as a crunchy snack.

Sawara – A Spanish mackerel native to the north Atlantic and Gulf of Mexico as well as to Japan's Inland Sea. Since it is a spawning fish, it is not suitable for *sashimi* due to freshwater parasites.

Sayaendo – A snow pea or sugar pea.

Sayaingen – A green bean or string bean.

Sayamame – A soybean. Also called *edamame*.

Sayori – A halfbeak or gar, a long, slender fish with a prominent lower jaw, native to tropical oceans and fresh water. Served as *sashimi* and *sunomono*, as well as in a variety of other Japanese dishes.

Sazae – A sea snail, also called turban shell or turbo, usually served steamed in the shell or sliced and marinated.

Seburuga – The Japanese pronunciation of Sevruga caviar.

Seigo – A young sea bass with a long body and spiny fins, native to the north Atlantic.

Sembei – A general term for crispy Japanese rice crackers flavored with soy sauce or other seasonings, a popular snack.

Sencha – High-quality Japanese green tea made from young, tender leaves.

Sengiri – A general term for any kind of shredded ingredient, such as cabbage or *daikon* radish.

Seri – A water dropwort native to the marshes of Japan. Often served pickled or in a variety of Japanese dishes.

Shako – A mantis shrimp, a gray, flat, rugged crustacean, popular in Japan but uncommon in the U.S. Also a term for a giant clam native to the southern islands of Japan.

Shari – Another word for *sushi* rice.

Shiba ebi – A white shrimp.

Shichimi togarashi – A blend of seven spices, including red pepper (*togarashi*), ground *sansho*, pepper pods, dried mandarin orange peel, black hemp seeds or white poppy seeds, *nori* seaweed bits, and white sesame seeds.

Shiira – A dolphinfish, a lean, ocean-going fish native to the warm Pacific waters, especially near Hawaii. Sometimes eaten as *sashimi*, also cooked in oil or salted and dried.

Shiitake – A Japanese mushroom, cultivated on the logs of the *shii* tree, a chestnut-oak, widely popular for a variety of Japanese dishes. Available fresh or dried.

Shijimi – A freshwater clam, native to coastal lakes and rivers. Often added to *miso* soup.

Shima – A prefix meaning 'striped,' usually referring to fish such as *shima aji*.

Shima aji – A striped yellowjack or mackerel with red striped white flesh, native to the western Atlantic and Gulf of Mexico.

Shime saba – Marinated mackerel.

Shimeji – A pale, delicate mushroom, also called *honshimeji*.

Shimofuri – A general term for blanching ingredients in boiling water.

Shinachiku – A pickled bamboo shoot.

Shinko – A young gizzard shad. Also a general term for Japanese pickles.

Shinko maki – *Makizushi* rolls filled with bright yellow pickled *daikon* radish. Also called *Takuan-maki*, named for Takuan Soho, the Buddhist monk who is credited with its invention.

Shio – The Japanese word for salt.

Shiokara – Salt-cured fish, shellfish and their entrails, with squid being the most popular.

Shioyaki – A general term for salt-grilling.

Shiozuke – A general term for a salt pickle, the most common method of pickling vegetables.

Shira ae – A cooked salad mixed in a *tofu* dressing.

Shirako – Codfish sperm sacs filled with soft white roe.

Shirasu – A young sardine, usually boiled, dried and used for simmered broths.

Shira-uo – A whitebait, a young herring, sprat, or smelt, usually cooked whole and used in many different dishes.

Shiro maguro – Albacore tuna. Its name means 'white tuna' and is the same albacore found in higher priced cans of tuna at the supermarket. Known also as *binnaga*, and scientifically as *Thunnus alalunga*, reaching a maximum weight of only about 40 lbs. (18 kg.), *shiro maguro* is peachy or rosy in color when served raw as *sushi*, although exposure to air quickly renders its delicate, translucent flesh darker and more opaque. As a result, some *sushi* chefs serve *shiro maguro* lightly seared on the outside. The fatty underbelly of *shiro maguro* is called *binjo*.

Shiromi – Any of a number of white-fleshed fish, including *tai*, *hirame*, etc.

Shirouo – An ice goby, a small coastal fish with a large head, a tapered body and spiny fins. Sometimes served and swallowed whole while still alive.

Shiru – A general term for any kind of soup or sauce.

Shishamo – A smelt, a small, silver ocean or freshwater fish native to cold northern waters. Often served grilled whole with roe intact.

Shiso – A perilla, or beefsteak plant, a piquant leaf, in both green and red varieties, widely used in Japanese cuisine as a garnish, flavoring agent, pickled, or fried *tempura*-style.

Shisonomi – A *shiso* bud, used as a garnish, or in salads or fried *tempura*-style.

Shita birame – A sole, a flatfish with a migrating eye, native to warm waters.

Shochu – A strong, distilled spirit made from rice or potatoes.

Shoga – Ginger root, an important component in Japanese cuisine, both fresh and pickled, always served as an accompaniment to *sushi*.

Shokuji – A Japanese meal.

Shokunin – A master *sushi* chef.

Shoyu – Fermented soy sauce made with soybeans, wheat and salt, an essential component of every Japanese meal.

Shiro goma – White sesame seeds.

Shun – The high season for any kind of seafood, vegetable or fruit.

Shungiku – A chrysanthemum, the national flower of Japan as well as an important edible vegetable.

Shuto – Salted bonito entrails.

Sobazushi – *Sushi* made with buckwheat *soba* noodles instead of vinegared rice.

Soramame – A fava bean, sometimes served in the pod as a snack, or as an ingredient in other dishes.

Sosu – A Japanese term for Worchestershire sauce. Also called *usuta sosu*.

Sozai – A general term for a side dish of any kind. Also called *osozai* or *okazu*.

Spider roll* – *Makizushi* roll filled with softshell crab *tempura*.

Su – A general term for unseasoned rice vinegar.

Sudachi – A Japanese citron, a bitter orange.

Sugaki – Oysters marinated in vinegar. A *sunomono* appetizer, often served with *ponzu* dipping sauce.

Sugatazushi – A *sushi* preparation technique in which the original form of the fish is represented, with the entrails removed, the flesh, head and tails left intact, marinated in salt and vinegar and the abdominal cavity filled with *sushi* rice.

Sugukina – A Japanese turnip, often served pickled, especially Kyoto-style.

Suikuchi – A general term for any fragrant food or ingredient.

Suimono – A general term for any kind of clear soup.

Sujiko – Salmon roe in the sac, preserved with salt or pickled with *sake*.

Suizenji nori – A rare form of blue-green algae used to make *nori* sheets or preserved in brine for an accompaniment to *sashimi* or in *sunomono* or soup.

Suketodara – An Alaskan pollack, also called *mentai*, a codfish native to northern waters, especially valued for its roe. Also spelled *sukesodara*.

Sukimi – Bits of fish scraped from the bones, used in *makizishi*, especially in reference to tuna.

Sumashi-jiru – A general term for a clear soup.

Sumibiyaki – A general term for charcoal grilling.

Sumi ika – A grilled squid or cuttlefish.

Sumiso – White *miso* mixed with rice vinegar, a dressing commonly used for freshwater fish. Also called *koromo*.

Sunomono – A salad dressed with vinegar. Its name literally means 'vinegared things' and may include a wide variety of vegetables and bits of minced seafood, often served as a complimentary appetizer at *sushi* bars.

Suppon – A soft-shelled snapping turtle indigenous to Japan, served as *sashimi* or deep-fried. Also used to make soup stock.

Surimi – A fine fish paste. Also called *kamaboko* or *chikuwa*.

Surume ika – A dried squid, served toasted and cut into thin strips.

Sushi – Any of a large number of Japanese seafoods, vegetables and various other ingredients prepared in combination with vinegared rice.

Sushi maki – A variety of *sushi* composed of vinegared rice and bits of fish or seafood, wrapped cigar-style in a sheet of toasted seaweed paper called *nori*, and sliced into bite-sized pieces. Also called *makizushi*.

Sushi tempura – *Makizushi* rolls, usually California rolls, dipped in batter and deep-fried *tempura*-style.

Suzuke – A vinegar pickle, *tsukemono*.

Suzuna – A Japanese turnip, often used in pickles and other vegetable dishes.

Suzushiro – An old name for *daikon* radish.

Suzuki – A sea bass, a large, firm white-fleshed fish, often served as *sashimi* or *sushi*.

Tachi-uo – An Atlantic cutlassfish, a long, slender scaleless fish with sharp teeth and a wispy tail, served as *sashimi*, *sunomono* and other styles of preparation.

Tade – A Japanese water pepper, both green and red, used as a flavor enhancer for fish, and also as an ingredient in dipping sauces. The red variety is also a strong coloring agent, especially for pickled red ginger and sour plums.

Tai – A sea bream native to the sea surrounding Japan, highly valued for its delicate, translucent flesh, usually served very thinly sliced. Because its name also means 'congratulations,' it is a popular choice for celebratory meals. The word *tai* is also used to refer to red snapper or porgy.

Tairagi – A razor-shell clam, also called fan shell, pen shell or sea pen, valued for its adductor muscle, which is served as *sashimi* or *sunomono*.

Taisho ebi – A plump, fleshy shrimp.

Taiyaki – A sponge cake molded in the shape of a sea bream, served at children's celebrations.

Taka no tsume – Cayenne pepper, a commonly used spice for certain types of *sushi* and many other Japanese dishes.

Takenoko – A bamboo shoot, widely cultivated in Japan and an essential element for many Japanese dishes, especially pickles and *sunomono*.

Tako – An octopus, an eight tentacled cephalopod that turns a rosy purple when cooked. Usually served marinated, grilled or as *nigiri sushi*.

Tako-su – Octopus marinated in rice wine vinegar and mixed with fresh cucumber, served as a *sunomono* appetizer.

Takuan zuke – Pickled *daikon* radish, bright yellow, crunchy, commonly served as a side dish or as *shinko maki* rolls. Also called *Takuan-maki*, named for Takuan Soho, the Buddhist monk who is credited with its invention.

Tamago – A hen's egg, widely used in Japanese cooking. Also refers to a sweet egg omelet, sliced thin and used as a topping for *nigiri sushi*.

Tamago su – An egg dissolved in rice vinegar.

Tamagoyaki – An egg omelet seasoned with soy sauce and *mirin*, sliced thin and used as a topping for *nigiri sushi*.

Tamari – Soy sauce brewed without wheat.

Tanpopo – A dandelion, widely used in Japanese vegetable dishes.

Tara – A codfish, a mild, white-fleshed spawning fish native to cold northern waters, sometimes served as *sashimi*.

Tarabagani – A king crab native to northern waters. Often used for *sunomono* and other seafood salads.

Tarako – Cod roe, pale yellow, compact eggs of the codfish. Also called *mentaiko*.

Tare – A general term for any kind of thick sauce, usually made with sweetened soy sauce or *miso*.

Tataki – A preparation method for fish, finely minced and seasoned with ginger, onion and *shiso*. Also refers to bonito or beef, lightly seared on the outside, sliced thin and served with ginger and soy sauce.

Tatami iwashi – Sun-dried sardines.

Tazuna sushi – A *makisuzhi* roll with thin slices of fish wrapped around the outside, often called a Rainbow roll, *Geisha* roll, Dragon roll or Caterpillar roll.

Teishoku – A Japanese set meal, several items for a fixed price.

Tekka – A *sushi* term for tuna, especially when used as a filling for *makizushi*.

Tekka don – Thin slices of raw tuna over rice.

Tekka maki – *Makizushi* rolls filled with raw tuna. Much like the origin of the sandwich, *tekkamaki* was Japan's first 'fast food,' prepared for gamblers in dice casinos called *tekkaba*, so that they could eat with one hand and roll dice with the other. And thus the tasty treat called *tekkamaki* got its name.

Tekkappa maki – A combination of both tuna and cucumber rolls.

Temaki – *Te* means 'hand,' and *temaki* is composed of any of the same ingredients as those used to form *maki* rolls, but instead of being snugly rolled into long cylinders, the filling is wrapped in a loosely filled cone of *nori*.

Tempura – Seafood and vegetables dipped in a light batter and deep-fried to a crisp golden brown, served with *tentsuyu* sauce, grated *daikon* and ginger root. Sometimes used as a filling for *makizushi*.

Tentsuyu – A dipping sauce made with *dashi*, soy sauce, and *mirin*, served with *tempura*.

Teriyaki – A method of grilling meats and fish with a thick glaze of soy sauce, *mirin*, *sake* and sugar, which gives the cooked food a lustrous brown sheen.

Tobiko – Flying fish roe, tiny, crunchy, bright orange fish eggs, usually served as *gunkan-maki*, sometimes topped with a quail egg yolk, or used as a delicate garnish for other types of *sushi*.

Tobi-tama – *Gunkan-maki* filled with *tobiko* topped with a quail egg yolk.

Tobiuo – A flying fish, a large, ocean-going fish with wing-like fins that enable it to glide in the air for short distances.

Tofu – Soybean curd, made by boiling ground soybeans with water, and then shaped into blocks. Available in many styles and textures, and used in a wide variety of Japanese dishes, or it may be eaten by itself with various sauces and toppings.

Togarashi – Cayenne pepper, available in whole dried pods, or also ground into powder and used as a component of a spice blend called *shichimi togarashi*.

Tokkyu – A premium-grade *sake*, usually served only on special occasions.

Tokobushi – A Japanese abalone.

Tokoroten – Thin, gelatinous seaweed noodles mixed with soy sauce and vinegar, served cold as an appetizer.

Tora no me roll – Broiled squid body filled with salmon, avocado and spring onion, but no rice. Its name means 'Eye of the Tiger.'

Torigai – A cockle shell, a fan-shaped mollusk, often served as *nigiri sushi* or in *sunomono*.

Toro – The rich, fatty, buttery underbelly of the tuna, the rarest and choicest cut of the fish and an expensive *sushi* bar delicacy. Also called *otoro*.

Tororu – A term for finely grated ingredients.

Tsubu – A Japanese sea snail native to Hokkaido.

Tsukemono – A general term for Japanese pickles, of which there are a wide variety of regional styles, ingredients and preparation methods.

Tsukemono maki – *Makizushi* rolls filled with various Japanese pickles.

Tsukimi – A general term for adding a raw egg yolk as a topping for many different Japanese dishes, including a quail's egg as a topping for *gunkan maki*.

Tsukudani – A salty-sweet mixture of seafood, vegetables or both, seasoned with soy sauce and *mirin*.

Tsumamimono – Snack foods served with alcoholic beverages.

Ume shiso – A mixture of plum paste and *shiso* leaf, sometimes used as a filling for *makizushi*. Also called *umejiso*.

Umeboshi – A pickled sour plum, very salty and tart, used as a filling for *onigiri* rice balls, and as a flavoring agent for other Japanese dishes.

Umeshu – A strong spirit flavored with pickled sour plum.

Unagi – A freshwater eel, a predatory, snake-like fish with smooth, slippery skin. Always served toasted, smoked or pickled, and especially popular as a topping for *nigiri sushi* or a filling in *makizushi* rolls.

Unagi maki – *Makizushi* filled with toasted eel.

Unagi no kimo – Eel entrails.

Unaju – Grilled eel glazed with a rich dark sauce served as a topping for pressed rice in a lacquered box.

Unakyu maki – *Makizushi* rolls filled with grilled *unagi*.

Uni – The reproductive glands of a sea urchin, a mustard-colored shellfish with a strong flavor. Usually served as *gunkan-maki*, an expensive seasonal delicacy.

Uoshoyu – The Japanese name for Asian fish sauce. Also called *nam pla*, *nuoc mam* or *patis*.

Uramaki – *Makizushi* rolls with the rice on the outside and only the fish and/or vegetable filling on the inside.

Uroko – Fish scales.

Uruka – Sweetfish entrails prepared as *shiokara*.

Usukuchi shoyu – Light soy sauce.

Usugiri – A general term for thinly sliced ingredients.

Usu-zukuri – A method of preparing *sashimi*, especially *fugu* and *hirame*, in which paper-thin slices of translucent white fish are decoratively arranged on a plate.

Utsubo – A moray eel, a snake-like, carnivorous ocean fish.

Uzura-tamago – A quail egg, often used as a topping on *gunkan maki*.

Wakame – A delicate seaweed, most commonly available dried, used in a variety of dishes such as *miso* soup and *sunomono*.

Wakasagi – A pond smelt, a small silvery fish that migrates between fresh and salt water. Often served in vinegar or deep-fried *tempura* style.

Warabi – A wild bracken often used in Japanese pickles and vegetable dishes.

Warasa – The youngest yellowtail.

Wasabi – A spicy root vegetable in the horseradish family, typically served finely grated or powdered and mixed into a paste as an accompaniment for *sushi* and *sashimi*.

Wata – The entrails of various types of seafood, commonly used to make *shiokara*.

Watarigani – A blue crab native to the eastern coastal waters of Japan.

Yaki – A general term for any kind of grilled food.

Yakidofu- Broiled or grilled *tofu*.

Yakimono – Broiled or grilled foods.

Yakinori- Toasted seaweed paper.

Yakumi – Any kind of strongly flavored seasoning, such as *shichimi togarashi*, grated *daikon*, or spring onion.

Yama fugu – *Sashimi* of *konnyaku*, a gray, rubbery, gelatinous paste made from the root of the devil's tongue plant.

Yama-imo – A Japanese yam or mountain potato. Also called *taro*, used to make Hawaiian *poi*, as well as a variety of traditional Japanese dishes.

Yama-imo ume – Mountain potato topped with sour plum paste, sometimes used as a filling in *makizushi* or *temaki* rolls.

Yamakake – Raw tuna mixed with mountain potato, *wasabi*, quail egg, and seaweed.

Yama-kake maki – *Makizushi* rolls filled with raw tuna and mountain potato.

Yari ika – A long-finned squid.

Yasai – A general term for cultivated vegetables.

Yasai maki – *Makizushi* rolls filled with vegetables such as carrots, cucumber, mountain potato, burdock root, etc.

Yomogi – A mugwort plant used in a variety of vegetable dishes.

Yuago – A gourd from which *kanpyo* is made.

Yudofu – Boiled *tofu* served with soy sauce, grated ginger, *daikon*, bonito flakes and green onion.

Yurine – A lily root, used in a variety of Japanese dishes.

Yuzu – A citron, a Japanese lemon used as a flavoring agent in many Japanese dishes, especially *ponzu* dipping sauce.

Zabon – A shaddock or pomelo.

Zarigani – A Japanese freshwater crayfish, usually served cooked.

Zenmai – A royal fern or fiddlehead fern used in many Japanese dishes.

Zensai – A general term for small appetizers.

Zuke – Raw tuna dipped in soy sauce.

Zuwaigani – A snow crab native to the Sea of Japan, served as *sashimi, sunomono* and *tempura*

* These creations originated outside of Japan, but are referred to by the Japanese with the English terms.

A Reverse Glossary

Abalone – *Awabi* – An abalone, a large gastropod with a nacreous shell, native to the north Pacific, a rare seasonal delicacy, especially for *sashimi*. Often commercially cultivated.

Abalone – *Tokobushi* – A Japanese abalone.

Adductor muscle – *Kaibashira* – The adductor muscle of a shellfish, such as scallop, or clam, often served as *sashimi*, *sushi*, or *sunomono*.

Albacore – *Mebachi maguro* – An albacore, a smaller white tuna native to tropical waters, most commonly available as canned tuna, but also served as *sushi*.

Albacore tuna – *Bincho maguro* – An albacore, also called *shiro maguro* (white tuna), with light pink flesh, often served seared on the outside.

Albacore tuna – *Shiro maguro* – Albacore tuna. Its name means 'white tuna' and is the same albacore found in higher priced cans of tuna at the supermarket. Known also as *binnaga*, and scientifically as *Thunnus alalunga*.

Amberjack – *Kanpachi* – An amberjack, also spelled *kampachi*, several types of copper–colored fish, native to warm tropical waters.

Anchovy – *Katakuchi–iwashi* – An anchovy, a tiny Mediterranean or tropical fish, best eaten raw with ginger and soy sauce, usually available canned or salted.

Appetizers – *Zensai* – A general term for small appetizers.

Ark Shell – A red clam, a burrowing mollusk, also called *peponita*, cockle or ark shell, with tender, rosy flesh, often eaten raw.

Ark shell mantle – *Himo* – The fringe or mantle of an ark shell.

Aspidistra – *Baran* – Aspidistra, an edible evergreen plant with large leaves, often grown as a houseplant.

Bamboo leaf – *Sasa* – Bamboo leaf.

Bamboo pickle – *Menma* – Pickled bamboo shoot.

Bamboo pickle – *Shinachiku* – A pickled bamboo shoot.

Bamboo shoot – *Nemagaritake* – A Chinese bamboo shoot, used in many Japanese dishes.

Bamboo shoot – *Takenoko* – A bamboo shoot, widely cultivated in Japan and an essential element for many Japanese dishes, especially pickles and *sunomono*.

Barracuda – *Kamasu* – A barracuda, a carnivorous marine fish with a cylindrical body and large mouth with a protruding lower jaw and long teeth.

Batter – *Koromo* – A general term for dressings and batters used to coat foods.

Battered foods – *Tempura* – Seafood and vegetables dipped in a light batter and deep–fried to a crisp golden brown, served with *tentsuyu* sauce, grated *daikon* and ginger root. Sometimes used as a filling for *makizushi*.

Battleship sushi – *Gunkan-maki* – Its name means 'battleship,' and *gunkan-maki* is another type of *nori* roll, in which the narrow strip of seaweed paper extends slightly beyond the top of the ball of vinegared rice, creating a shallow niche to hold a small serving of a soft ingredient such as fish roe, sea urchin, or minced shellfish.

Battleship sushi – *Kakomi sushi* – Another name for *gunkan maki* or *funamori*.

Bay scallop – *Itayagi* – A small bay scallop, native to coastal Japan and other parts of the world.

Bean sprouts – *Moyashi* – Bean sprouts.

Beef slices – *Kobe gyutataki* – *Kobe* beef lightly seared on the outside and still raw inside. A cool weather delicacy.

Beefsteak plant – *Aojiso* – A *shiso* leaf, a perilla, also known as the beefsteak plant, a member of the mint family, used as a garnish for *sushi* and *sashimi*, and also fried *tempura*–style.

Beefsteak plant – *Shiso* – A perilla, or beefsteak plant, a piquant leaf, in both green and red varieties, widely used in Japanese cuisine as a garnish, flavoring agent, pickled, or fried *tempura*-style.

Beer – *Biru* – The Japanese pronunciation of beer.

Beluga caviar – *Beruga* – The Japanese pronunciation of Beluga caviar, sturgeon eggs.

Beverage – *Inryo* – A general term for Japanese beverages.

Bill – *Oaiso* – The check or bill in a *sushi* restaurant.

Bitter Orange Vinegar – *Dadaisu* – Bitter orange vinegar flavored with Seville orange.

Black porgy – *Kuro dai* – A black porgy, a meaty fish native to warm coastal waters, not served as *sushi* or *sashimi* because of its strong fishy smell.

Black sesame seeds – *Kuro goma* – Black sesame seeds, used as a garnish on some kinds of *sushi*.

Blackfish – *Mejina* – A large scaled blackfish, native to coastal northern waters, and a popular choice for *sashimi*.

Blanch – *Shimofuri* – A general term for blanching ingredients in boiling water.

Blended miso – *Awasemiso* – A blended *miso*, highly favored, for making *miso* soup.

Blowfish – *Fugu* – A blowfish, globefish or pufferfish, with a spiny body that can inflate with air or water when threatened. Although a deadly toxin is contained in its liver and ovaries, it is nevertheless popular as an edible delicacy when properly prepared.

Blue crab – *Gazami* – A blue crab, also called *watarigani*, native to the coastal waters of Japan.

Blue crab – *Watarigani* – A blue crab native to the eastern coastal waters of Japan.

Blue goby – *Mutsugoro* – A blue spotted goby native to the coastal waters of Japan. Usually served grilled.

Blue king crab – *Hanasakigani* – A blue king crab, native to the waters surrounding the northern waters of Hokkaido.

Blue marlin – *Makajiki* – A blue marlin, an ocean–going fish with a long, pointed snout.

Blue sprat – *Kibinago* – A banded blue sprat, a small sardine–like fish native to European waters. Usually available smoked or canned.

Bluefin tuna – *Hobo* – A bluefin tuna, the largest variety reaches 1,500 lbs. (680 kg.), migrates between tropical and polar seas.

Bluefin tuna – *Minami-maguro* – A southern bluefin tuna.

Bluefish – *Mutsu* – A Japanese bluefish that feeds on smaller fish in shallow waters. Often served as *sashimi*.

Boat–wrap sushi – *Funamori* – Another name for *gunkanmaki*. Its name means 'boat wrap.'

Boiled food – *Ni–mono* – A general term for any kind of boiled or simmered food.

Boiled Soybean curd – *Yudofu* – Boiled *tofu* served with soy sauce, grated ginger, *daikon*, bonito flakes and green onion.

Bonito – *Katsuo* – A skipjack or bonito, an ocean–going variety of smaller tuna, native to both Atlantic and Pacific waters.

Bonito entrails – *Shuto* – Salted bonito entrails.

Bonito flakes – *Katsuo bushi* – Blocks of dried, smoked and cured bonito, which look like pieces of driftwood. When shaved into paper–thin flakes, *katsuo* may be used as a garnish, a flavoring agent and most importantly as a base for *dashi*, the most common Japanese soup stock.

Bonito shavings – *Keshinomi* – Delicate dried smoked bonito shavings used for garnish, flavoring, and as a base for *dashi* soup stock.

Botan shrimp – *Botan ebi* – A botan shrimp, sweet and translucent. Sometimes served with its own blue roe.

Boxed sushi – *Bento* – A boxed meal of rice, pickles, and certain types of *sushi*, often taken to school or work, and widely sold to travelers as *ekiben* in railway stations. *Makunouchi* is a common style, while *shokado* is formal and elegant.

Bracken – *Warabi* – A wild bracken often used in Japanese pickles and vegetable dishes.

Brown algae – *Arame* – A mild brown ocean algae, most commonly cooked with root vegetables as a side dish.

Brown rice vinegar – *Genmai su* – Brown rice vinegar.

Brown rice vinegar – *Kuro-su* – Brown rice vinegar.

Brown seaweed – *Hijiki* – A dark, brown seaweed that turns black when dried.

Brown seaweed – *Mozuku* – Delicate, dark brown seaweed often served as *sunomono* appetizers.

Brown striped mackerel – *Muroaji* – A brown–striped mackerel native to Japan. Often served as *sashimi* or *sushi*.

Buckwheat noodle sushi – *Sobazushi* – *Sushi* made with buckwheat *soba* noodles instead of vinegared rice.

Burdock root – *Gobo* – A burdock, a bitter root vegetable, often mixed with carrot in a dish called *kinpira gobo*.

Burdock root and carrot salad – *Kinpira gobo* – A dish of burdock root and carrot marinated in rice wine sweetened with *mirin* and sugar, and seasoned with chili pepper and soy sauce.

Buri – A yellowtail or amberjack, a mature type of *hamachi*, often served as *sashimi* or *nigiri sushi*, especially popular at New Year celebrations.

Butterbur – *Fuki* – A butterbur plant, similar to rhubarb or celery, commonly used for pickles.

Butterfish – *Ibodai* – A butterfish, a slippery, scaleless fish native to North Atlantic coastal waters.

California roll – *Makizushi* roll filled with crab, avocado and cucumber. By far the most popular specialty *makizushi* rolls in the U.S., their invention is attributed to Itamae-san Mashita of Tokyo Kaikan Restaurant of Los Angeles, which is no longer in operation. The California roll has undergone many evolutions since its invention in the early 1970s, most are now made with the rice on the outside, and garnished with sesame seeds or flying fish roe.

Calpis – A sweet soft drink derived from milk, similar in taste to barley water.

Carp – *Funa* – A crucian carp, a lake–dwelling goldfish, most commonly used to make *sashimi* and Osaka–style pressed *sushi*.

Carp – *Koi* – A Japanese carp, a lean, bony freshwater fish, often kept as decorative specimens in garden ponds.

Carrot – *Ninjin* – A carrot, a term for both western varieties as well as native Japanese carrots, widely used in many Japanese dishes.

Carrot and burdock root salad – *Kinpira gobo* – A dish of burdock root and carrot marinated in rice wine sweetened with *mirin* and sugar, and seasoned with chili pepper and soy sauce.

Caterpillar roll – *Makizushi* roll with thin slices of raw fish and avocado wrapped around the outside of a California roll. Another name for Rainbow roll, *Geisha* roll, or Dragon roll.

Catfish – *Kajika* – A bullhead catfish, a freshwater fish with a large head and long whiskers.

Catfish – *Namazu* – A catfish, usually served grilled or *tempura*–style and only in specialty restaurants.

Caviar – *Kyabia* – The Japanese pronunciation of caviar.

Cayenne pepper – *Taka no tsume* – Cayenne pepper, a commonly used spice for certain types of *sushi* and many other Japanese dishes.

Cayenne pepper – *Togarashi* – Cayenne pepper, available in whole dried pods, or also ground into powder and used as a component of a spice blend called *shichimi togarashi*.

Char – *Iwana* – A char, any of several small–scaled trout, native to cold streams.

Char – *Kawamasu* – A brook trout or char, originally from North America and introduced to Japan. Usually served cooked.

Charcoal grilling – *Sumibiyaki* – A general term for charcoal grilling.

Check – *Oaiso* – The check or bill in a *sushi* restaurant.

Chef – *Shokunin* – A master *sushi* chef.

Chef's choice – *Omakase* – A request for the *sushi* chef to choose the *sushi* selection for the customer.

Cherry blossom viewing – *Hanami* – Cherry blossom season, a time when *sushi* is especially popular as a traditional food for flower viewing parties.

Chinese cabbage – *Hakusai* – Chinese cabbage, often used in vinegared dishes called *tsukemono*.

Chives – *Asatsuki* – Chives, often served as a garnish for *fugu sashimi*.

Chives – *Nira* – Chinese chives, an important component of *gyoza* pot stickers.

Chrysanthemum – *Shungiku* – A chrysanthemum, the national flower of Japan as well as an important edible vegetable.

Chutoro maki – *Makizushi* rolls filled with semi–fatty tuna.

Citron – *Daidai*– A bitter Japanese citrus fruit, also called Seville orange. Its juice is mixed with soy sauce to make *ponzu*.

Citron – *Yuzu* – A citron, a Japanese lemon used as a flavoring agent in many Japanese dishes, especially *ponzu* dipping sauce.

Clam – *Hamaguri* – A clam, usually served steamed or fried as *yaki hamaguri*, and rarely served raw.

Clam – *Shijimi* – A freshwater clam, native to coastal lakes and rivers. Often added to *miso* soup.

Clear soup – *Suimono* – A general term for any kind of clear soup.

Clear soup – *Sumashi–jiru* – A general term for a clear soup.

Cloud ear mushroom – *Kikurage* – A dried cloud ear mushroom, served in *sunomono* appetizers and other vegetable dishes.

Cockle – A red clam, a burrowing mollusk, also called *peponita*, cockle or ark shell, with tender, rosy flesh, often eaten raw.

Cockle shell – *Torigai* – A cockle shell, a fan–shaped mollusk, often served as *nigiri sushi* or in *sunomono*.

Cod – *Komai* – A yellow cod, a lean white fish native to the north Atlantic.

Codfish – *Tara* – A codfish, a mild, white–fleshed spawning fish native to cold northern waters. Sometimes served as *sashimi*.

Codfish roe – *Tarako* – Cod roe, pale yellow, compact eggs of the codfish. Also called *mentaiko*.

Codfish sperm sac – *Shirako* – Codfish sperm sacs filled with soft white roe.

Coho salmon – *Ginzake* – A small coho salmon, native to the Great Lakes and the coastal waters of the north Pacific.

Cold tofu – *Hiyayako* – A block of cold *tofu* topped with grated ginger and spring onion.

Conch – *Horagai* – A conch, a spiral–shelled gastropod, native to warm tropical waters, with firm, mildly flavored white flesh, served as *sashimi* and *sushi*. Also used in vinegared *sunomono* appetizers.

Condiment – *Chomiryo* – The Japanese word for 'seasoning' or 'condiment.'

Congealed food – *Nikogori* – A general term for congealed food.

Conger eel – *Hamo* – A conger eel or pike conger native to Japan, very bony and always served cooked. Often used for *oshizushi*, Osaka–style pressed *sushi*.

Cooked rice – *Gohan* – The Japanese word for plain cooked rice. Also the word for meal.

Cooking – *Ryori* – A general term for cooking or cuisine of any kind.

Cooking wine – *Mirin* – A special type of sweet rice wine used only for cooking.

Crab – *Kani* – A crab, any of several varieties, always served cooked, and often substituted with imitation crab made from whitefish paste.

Crab entrails – *Kani miso* – The brown entrails inside a boiled crab shell, valued as a delicacy in Japan, straight from the shell or prepared in a sauce of rice wine, sugar and egg.

Crackers – *Sembei* – A general term for crispy Japanese rice crackers flavored with soy sauce or other seasonings. A popular snack.

Crayfish – *Zarigani* – A Japanese freshwater crayfish, usually served cooked.

Cucumber – *Kappa* – A *sushi* term for fresh cucumber, named for the *kappa*, a mythical water genie from Japanese folklore who is said to be fond of cucumbers.

Cucumber – *Kyuri* – A Japanese cucumber, smaller than U.S. varieties and without a large seed core. Most commonly used for pickles and *sunomono* appetizers.

Cucumber rolls – *Kappa maki* – *Makizushi* filled with strips of fresh cucumber.

Cucumber salad – *Morokyu* – Sliced cucumber marinated in unfiltered soy sauce.

Cuisine – *Ryori* – A general term for cooking or cuisine of any kind.

Cutlassfish – *Tachi-uo* – An Atlantic cutlassfish, a long, slender scaleless fish with sharp teeth and a wispy tail, served as *sashimi*, *sunomono* and in other styles of preparation.

Dandelion – *Tanpopo* – A dandelion, widely used in Japanese vegetable dishes.

Deep fried seaweed rolls – *Sushi tempura* – *Makizushi* rolls, usually California roll, dipped in batter and deep–fried *tempura*-style.

Deep-fried fish paste – *Satsuma-age* – Deep fried fish paste, a Tokyo favorite. Also called *age-kamaboko*.

Deep-Fried Foods – *Agedashi* – Deep-fried foods served with soy sauce, grated ginger and shredded *daikon*.

Deep-Fried Foods – *Agemono* – Deep-fried foods such as *tempura*.

Deep-Fried Tofu – *Agedofu* – Deep-fried *tofu*.

Delicacies – *Chinmi* – A Japanese term used to describe a rare delicacy, the three most prized being *uni, konowata* and *karasumi*.

Devil's tongue gelatin slices – *Yama fugu* – *Sashimi* of kon-nyaku, a gray, rubbery, gelatinous paste made from the root of the devil's tongue plant.

Devil's tongue gelatin – *Konnyaku* – The root of the devil's tongue plant, a gray, rubbery, gelatinous paste sold in blocks or strands. Used to make a variety of Japanese dishes.

Dipping sauce – *Ponzu* – A Japanese dipping sauce, soy sauce flavored with citron.

Dipping sauce for tempura – *Tentsuyu* – A dipping sauce made with *dashi*, soy sauce, and *mirin*, served with *tempura*.

Dolphinfish – *Shiira* – A dolphinfish, a lean, ocean–going fish native to the warm Pacific waters, especially near Hawaii. Sometimes eaten as *sushi* and also cooked in oil or salted and dried.

Dragon roll – *Makizushi* roll with thin slices of raw fish and avocado wrapped around the outside of a California roll. Another name for Rainbow roll, *Geisha* roll, or Caterpillar roll.

Dressing – *Koromo* – A general term for dressings and batters used to coat foods.

Dressing – *Sanbaizu* – A mixture of vinegar, soy sauce and *mirin*, used as a dressing for seafood and vegetables.

Dried fish – *Mirinboshi* – Any of a variety of small fish such as *aji*, butterflied, marinated in *mirin* and soy sauce and then dried.

Dried fish – *Niboshi* – Small dried fish, especially anchovies, commonly used for making soup stocks.

Dried fish paste – *Denbu* – Dried whitefish and shrimp paste, colored red and shredded, most commonly used in *futomaki* or as a topping for *chirashizushi*.

Dried foods – *Nishime* – Dried foods seasoned with soy sauce, ginger and *mirin*, often included in *bento* boxes or as special New Year dishes.

Dried gourd – *Kanpyo* – Dried strips of the *yugao* gourd, also known as calabash, a tropical American evergreen that produces large bottle–shaped gourds, used in many Japanese dishes.

Dried sardines – *Tatami iwashi* – Sun-dried sardines.

Dried sea kelp – *Oboro konbu* – Dried flakes of sea kelp, used as an ingredient for *sunomono*.

Dried squid – *Surume ika* – A dried squid, served toasted and cut into thin strips.

Dried whitefish – *Oboro* – Dried whitefish flakes, used as a filling for *makizushi* or as a topping for various Japanese dishes.

Dropwort – *Seri* – A water dropwort native to the marshes of Japan, often served pickled or in a variety of Japanese dishes.

Dynamite roll – *Makizushi* roll filled with spicy tuna, salmon, *hamachi,* etc.

Eel – *Unagi* – A freshwater eel, a predatory, snake–like fish with smooth, slippery skin, always served toasted, smoked or pickled. Especially popular as a topping for *nigiri sushi* or a filling in *makizushi* rolls.

Eel entrails – *Unagi no kimo* – Freshwater eel entrails.

Eel roll – *Unagi maki*– Makizushi filled with toasted freshwater eel.

Eel rolls – *Unakyu maki* – *Makizushi* rolls filled with grilled *unagi*.

Egg – *Tamago* – A hen's egg, widely used in Japanese cooking. Also refers to a sweet egg omelet, sliced thin and used as a topping for *nigiri sushi*.

Egg custard – *Chawan mushi* – A savory steamed egg custard served in a *chawan* tea mug.

Egg omelet – *Datemaki* – A sweet rolled omelet made with eggs and whitefish. Especially popular at New Year celebrations.

Egg omelet – *Tamagoyaki* – An egg omelet seasoned with soy sauce and *mirin*, sliced thin and used as a topping for *nigiri sushi*.

Egg omelet rolls – *Noritama* – Egg omelet wrapped in *nori* seaweed paper.

Egg vinegar – *Tamago su* – An egg dissolved in rice vinegar.

Egg yolk topping – *Tsukimi* – A general term for adding a raw egg yolk as a topping for many different Japanese dishes, including a quail's egg as a topping for *gunkan maki*.

Eggplant – *Nasu* – A Japanese eggplant, often used to make pickles, or as a fresh ingredient in many other dishes.

Eggplant grilled – *Nasu yaki* – Broiled eggplant.

Eggplant pickle – *Nasu no tsukemono* – Pickled eggplant.

Egg–wrapped sushi – *Chakin-zushi* – *Sushi* rice wrapped in a thin egg omelet.

Entrails – *Motsu* – A general term for entrails or giblets, used to prepare many types of Japanese dishes.

Entrails – *Wata* – The entrails of various types of seafood, commonly used to make *shiokara*.

Eye of the Tiger roll – *Tora no me roll* – Broiled squid body filled with salmon, avocado and spring onion, but no rice. Its name means 'Eye of the Tiger.'

Fatty tuna – *Toro* – The rich, fatty, buttery underbelly of the tuna, the rarest and choicest cut of the fish and an expensive *sushi* bar delicacy. Also called *otoro*.

Fava beans – *Soramame* – A fava bean, sometimes served in the pod as a snack, or as an ingredient in other dishes.

Fermentation – *Hakko* – A general term for fermentation.

Fermentation starter – *Aspergillus* – A type of mold used to make *koji*, a starter for many fermented foods.

Fermentation starter – *Koji* – A fermentation starter. Grains or beans inoculated with Aspergillus mold and used as a starter for fermented foods such as *miso, tamari, shoyu, amazake, mirin* and rice vinegar.

Fermented soybean rolls – *Natto Maki* – *Makizushi* rolls filled with *natto*, sticky, stinky fermented soybeans.

Fermented soybeans – *Natto* – Fermented soybeans, sticky, stinky and definitely an acquired taste,. Often used as a filling for *makizushi*, or as an ingredient in many other Japanese dishes.

Filefish – *Hage* – A filefish or leather fish, a flat, narrow fish with leathery skin, native to warm waters. Often served as *sashimi*.

Filefish – *Kawahagi* – A filefish or leather fish, a flat, narrow fish with leathery skin, native to warm waters.

Fin muscle – *Engawa* – The small muscle around the fin of a flounder or halibut, or the meat surrounding the muscle in a scallop, a delicacy usually eaten raw.

Firefly squid – *Hotaru ika* – A firefly squid.

First course – *Mukozuke* – The first course of a Japanese meal. Often used to refer to *sashimi*.

Fish – *Sakana* – A general term for any kind of fish. Also a term for any kind of food that is traditionally served with *sake*.

Fish filled with rice – *Sugatazushi* – A *sushi* preparation technique in which the original form of the fish is represented, with the entrails removed, the flesh, head and tails left intact, marinated in salt and vinegar and the abdominal cavity filled with *sushi* rice.

Fish in soybean paste – *Saikyo-yaki* – Fish marinated in *miso* and seared outside, leaving the inside raw.

Fish meat – *Saku* – A block of fish meat.

Fish paste – *Itawasa* – *Kamaboko* fish paste, sliced and served with *wasabi* and soy sauce.

Fish paste – *Kamaboko* – A fish paste made with mild white fish, and molded into various shapes, most commonly imitation crab.

Fish paste – *Surimi* – A fine fish paste. Also called *kamaboko* or *chikuwa*.

Fish roe – *Gyoran* – A general term for fish roe.

Fish roll – *Tazuna sushi* – A *makisuzhi* roll with thin slices of fish wrapped around the outside. Often called a Rainbow roll, *Geisha* roll, Dragon roll or Caterpillar roll.

Fish sauce – *Gyosho* – The Japanese name for Asian fish sauce. Also called *nuoc mam*, *patis*, and *nam pla*.

Fish sauce – *Uoshoyu* – The Japanese name for Asian fish sauce. Also called *nam pla*, *nuoc mam* or *patis*.

Fish scales – *Uroko* – Fish scales.

Fish scrapings – *Sukimi* – Bits of fish scraped from the bones, used in *makizushi*, especially in reference to tuna.

Fish slices – *Sashimi* – Thin slices of raw fish, usually served with a garnish of grated *daikon* radish, *wasabi* paste, and soy sauce for dipping. Traditionally the first course of a *sushi* meal.

Fish topping – *Neta* – A *sushi* bar term for the fish topping in *nigiri sushi*.

Flatfish – *Kochi* – A flatfish, any of several varieties with a migrating eye and a flattened body, served as *sashimi* and *sushi*.

Flathead – *Megochi* – A big–eyed flathead, a bottom-dwelling fish with a flattened snout, native to the waters of Indonesia.

Flounder – *Hirame* – A flounder or halibut, a flat fish with delicate flesh and a migrating eye, native to the waters of North America and Europe.

Flounder – *Karei* – A halibut, plaice, flounder, or sand dab, a flatfish with a migrating eye, native to northern waters. Especially favored for *sashimi*.

Flying fish – *Tobiuo* – A flying fish, a large, ocean-going fish with wing-like fins that enable it to glide in the air for short distances.

Flying fish roe – *Tobiko* – Flying fish roe, tiny, crunchy, bright orange fish eggs, usually served as *gunkan-maki*. Sometimes topped with a quail egg yolk, or used as a delicate garnish for other types of *sushi*.

Flying fish roe with quail egg – *Tobi-tama* – *Gunkan-maki* filled with *tobiko* topped with a quail egg yolk.

Food arrangement – *Moritsuke* – The Japanese art of food arrangement.

Fragrant food – *Suikuchi* – A general term for any fragrant food or ingredient.

Freeze–dried tofu – *Koyadofu* – Freeze–dried *tofu* that becomes spongy and soft when reconstituted. Sometimes used as a filler for *makizushi*.

Fresh – *Nama* – A Japanese prefix that means fresh or raw. Used to describe foods and also draft beer.

Freshwater eel – *Unagi* – A freshwater eel, a predatory, snake–like fish with smooth, slippery skin. Always served toasted, smoked or pickled, and especially popular as a topping for *nigiri sushi* or a filling in *makizushi* rolls.

Fried Tofu Pouches – *Aburage* – Thin slices of deep-fried *tofu*, used to make *inarizushi*.

Gar – *Sayori* – A halfbeak or gar, a long, slender fish with a prominent lower jaw, native to tropical oceans and fresh water. Served as *sashimi* and *sunomono*, as well as in a variety of other Japanese dishes.

Garlic – *Ninniku* – Garlic, widely available in Japan but used in a limited number of Japanese dishes.

Geisha roll – *Makizushi* roll with thin slices of raw fish and avocado wrapped around the outside of a California roll. Also called Rainbow roll, Caterpillar roll, and Dragon roll.

Geoduck – *Mirugai* – A geoduck or horse-neck clam, a very large burrowing clam with a long, muscular foot, served sliced as *sushi*.

Geoduck – *Mirukui* – The original name for *mirugai*, a geoduck or horse-neck clam.

Giant roll – *Futomaki* – Much like *maki* rolls, *futomaki* is an oversized *nori* roll, filled with a colorful assortment of rice, cucumber, red ginger, pink fish cake, dried gourd, pickled yellow radish, and egg omelet. When sliced, the colorful ingredients inside form an attractive pattern in the center of each piece.

Ginger buds – *Myoga* – A type of ginger used for its buds and shoots rather than for its roots, fragrant and herbaceous rather than peppery, served in salads , or pickled as a garnish for grilled fish.

Ginger root – *Shoga* – Ginger root, an important component in Japanese cuisine, both fresh and pickled, always served as an accompaniment to *sushi*.

Ginger shoot – *Hajikami* – A ginger shoot, often served pickled.

Gizzard shad – *Kohada* – A Tokyo name for a gizzard shad, a herring-like spawning fish native to northern waters.

Gizzard shad – *Konoshiro* – A large gizzard shad, a herring-like spawning fish native to the north Atlantic. A popular fish for *sashimi* and *sushi*.

Gizzard shad – *Shinko* – A young gizzard shad. Also a general term for Japanese pickles.

Goby – *Haze* – A goby, a fish native to many waters including Tokyo Bay. Often served as *sashimi*.

Goby – *Shirouo* – An ice goby, a small coastal fish with a large head, a tapered body and spiny fins. Sometimes served and swallowed whole while still alive.

Gourd – *Yuago* – A gourd from which *kanpyo* is made.

Gourd rolls – *Kanpyo maki* – *Makizushi* rolls filled with pickled *kanpyo* gourd.

Grated ingredients – *Tororu* – A term for finely grated ingredients.

Grated radish – *Oroshi-wasabi* – Grated *wasabi* root.

Grated radish with red pepper – *Momiji-oroshi* – Grated *daikon* radish with red pepper.

Gray mullet – *Bora* – A gray mullet with a cylindrical body and a pair of feeders on its chin, native to warm coastal waters around the world. Sometimes served as *sashimi*.

Gray mullet roe – *Karasumi* – Gray mullet roe served dried and salted, one of Japan's three most prized delicacies.

Green bean – *Sayaingen* – A green bean or string bean.

Green laver – *Aonori* – Green laver, toasted seaweed flakes sprinkled on various foods as a condiment or seasoning.

Green onion slices – *Sarashi negi* – Thinly sliced green onion, used for *sushi* garnishes and in *ponzu* dipping sauce.

Green Tea – *Agari* – A Japanese *sushi*-bar term for freshly drawn green tea, a shortened form of *agaribana*, which means 'above all.'

Green tea – *Bancha* – Common Japanese green tea.

Green tea – *Ocha* – A general term for Japanese green tea.

Green tea – *Sencha* – High-quality Japanese green tea made from young, tender leaves.

Green tea for ceremony – *Matcha* – Powdered green tea used in the Japanese tea ceremony.

Greenling – *Hokke* – A greenling or mackerel, native to the northern Pacific. Usually served grilled.

Grilled eel pressed sushi – *Unaju* – Grilled eel glazed with a rich dark sauce served as a topping for pressed rice in a lacquered box.

Grilled food – *Yaki* – A general term for any kind of grilled food.

Grilled foods – *Yakimono* – Broiled or grilled foods.

Grilled soybean curd – *Yakidofu*– Broiled or grilled *tofu*.

Grilled squid – *Sumi ika* – A grilled squid or cuttlefish.

Grilling with soy glaze – *Teriyaki* – A method of grilling meats and fish with a thick glaze of soy sauce, *mirin*, *sake* and sugar, which gives the cooked food a lustrous brown sheen.

Grouper – *Hata* – A grouper, a bottom-dweller native to tropical seas.

Grunt fish – *Isaki* – A grunt fish, native to tropical seas, named for the grunting sound it makes. Often served as *sashimi*.

Halibut – *Hirame* – A flounder or halibut, a flat fish with delicate flesh and a migrating eye, native to the waters of North America and Europe.

Halibut – *Karei* – A halibut, plaice, flounder, or sand dab, a flatfish with a migrating eye, native to northern waters. Especially favored for *sashimi*.

Halibut – *Oyo* – A halibut, a large flatfish with a migrating eye, native to northern waters. Often served as *sashimi*. Also called *ohyo*.

Hand roll – *Temaki* – *Te* means 'hand,' and *temaki* is composed of any of the same ingredients as those used to form *maki* rolls, but instead of being snugly rolled into long cylinders, the filling is wrapped in a loosely filled cone of *nori*.

Hen clam – *Hokki gai* – A red-tipped surf clam, also called hen clam, off-white when served as *sashimi* and *sushi*, but turns bright pink when cooked.

Hen-of-the-wood – *Mai-take* – Hen-of-the-wood, a Japanese mushroom used in many dishes.

Herb – *Koso* – A general term for herbs, including water pepper, *shiso*, and trefoil.

Herring – *Iwashi* – A sardine or herring, small fish that swims in large schools, native to the coastal waters in many parts of the world. Sometimes served as *sashimi* or grilled. Usually available canned.

Herring – *Nishin* – A herring, native to the northern Atlantic and Pacific, usually available salted or pickled. Also valued for its roe.

Herring roe – *Kazunoko* – Herring roe, tiny, salty, bright yellow, compact herring eggs, often served at New Year celebrations.

High-class restaurant – *Ryotei* – A very high-class Japanese restaurant, with private rooms for patrons and a set menu specially designed by the chef.

Hiramasa – A gold-striped amberjack native to warm seas.

Hokkaido shrimp – *Hokkai ebi* – A shrimp native to the waters around the northern island of *Hokkaido*.

Home-brewed rice wine – *Doburoku* – Home-brewed *sake*. Thick, actively fermenting, and illegal.

Home-style sushi – *Okonomizushi* – Homestyle *nigiri sushi*.

Horse Mackerel – *Aji* – A horse mackerel or jack fish, often served as *sashimi*.

Horsehair crab – *Kegani* – A horsehair crab.

Horsemeat sashimi – *Basashi* – *Sashimi* of horsemeat, served with garlic and ginger-infused soy sauce. Especially popular in Kumamoto and Nagano.

Horse-neck clam – *Mirugai* – A geoduck or horse-neck clam, a very large burrowing clam with a long, muscular foot, served sliced as *sushi*.

Horse-neck clam – *Mirukui* – The original name for *mirugai*, a geoduck or horse-neck clam.

Horseradish paste – *Neri-wasabi* – Japanese horseradish paste.

Horseradish root – *Wasabi* – A spicy root vegetable in the horseradish family, typically served finely grated or powdered and mixed into a paste as an accompaniment for *sushi* and *sashimi*.

Hot Rice Beverage – *Amazake* – A hot beverage made from water, cooked rice and a thick fermenting starter called *koji*, sweetened and seasoned with ginger. A popular New Year beverage, and as a medicinal toddy for colds and sore throats.

Iced sashimi – *Arai* – A style of *sashimi* preparation in which the fish is immersed in ice water to freshen its flavor before serving.

Inside-out rolls – *Uramaki* – *Makizushi* rolls with the rice on the outside and only the fish and/or vegetable filling on the inside.

Jellyfish – *Kurage* – A jellyfish, usually served marinated in *sunomono* appetizers.

John Dory – *Matodai* – A John Dory, a fish with a large mouth and a distinctive black spot on its side, native to Japan's southern waters.

Kelp – *Konbu* – A large, thick, wide sea kelp native to the waters of northern Japan, sold in dried form. Most commonly used in making *dashi*, the most common soup stock, where it softens and expands to several times its size.

King crab – *Tarabagani* – A king crab native to northern waters. Often used for *sunomono* and other seafood salads.

Knot – *Musubi* – A decorative knot or tie for certain herbs and vegetables used as a garnish for Japanese food. Also a term for rice balls filled with fish, vegetables or pickles, sometimes wrapped in *nori*. Also called *o-nigiri*.

Lean Red Tuna – *Akami* – A cut of lean, red tuna from the upper and inner side of the fish near the spine.

Leather fish – *Hage* – A filefish or leather fish, a flat, narrow fish with leathery skin, native to warm waters. Often served as *sashimi*.

Leather fish – *Kawahagi* – A filefish or leather fish, a flat, narrow fish with leathery skin, native to warm waters.

Lemon – *Yuzu* – A citron, a Japanese lemon used as a flavoring agent in many Japanese dishes, especially *ponzu* dipping sauce.

Light soy sauce – *Usukuchi shoyu* – Light soy sauce.

Lily root – *Yurine* – A lily root, used in a variety of Japanese dishes.

Live fish – *Odorigui* – Tiny whitebait fish dressed with vinegar and soy sauce and served while still alive.

Live shrimp – *Odori* – Raw shrimp or langoustine prepared and served while still alive. Its name means 'dance.' Also called *odori ebi*.

Lobster – *Ise ebi* – A spiny lobster, a saltwater crustacean, usually served grilled at New Year celebrations.

Local specialty – *Ji mono* – A general term for items of local specialty, including fish, pickles, *sake*, etc.

Loofa gourd – *Hechima* – A loofa gourd, sometimes served in vinegared *sunomono* appetizers.

Lotus root – *Hasu* – Lotus root, also known as *renkon*.

Lotus root – *Renkon* – Lotus root, widely used in Japanese pickles and other dishes.

Lunch box – *Orizume* – A general term for food packed in a box lunch.

Lunchbox – *Bento* – A boxed meal of rice, pickles, and certain types of *sushi*, often taken to school or work, and widely sold to travelers as *ekiben* in railway stations. *Makunouchi* is a common style, while *shokado* is formal and elegant.

Mackerel – *Saba* – A mackerel, a small, oily, red-fleshed fish with silvery skin, native to the Atlantic, available seasonally. Usually served with ginger and spring onion.

Mackerel pike – *Sanma* – A mackerel pike, a freshwater fish with a long snout native to northern waters, served as *sashimi* and *sunomono* as well as in other dishes and types of preparations.

Mackerel sushi – *Sabazushi* – Mackerel *sushi*, a general term for any kind of *sushi* made with fresh raw mackerel.

Mandarin orange – *Mikan* – A mandarin orange or tangerine.

Mantis shrimp – *Shako* – A mantis shrimp, a gray, flat, rugged crustacean, popular in Japan but uncommon in the U.S. Also a term for a giant clam native to the southern islands of Japan.

Mantled Squid – *Aoriika* – A mantled squid, a ten-tentacled cephalopod with triangular fins.

Marinated mackerel – *Shime saba* – Marinated mackerel.

Marlin – *Makajiki* – A blue marlin, an ocean-going fish with a long, pointed snout.

Meal – *Gohan* – The Japanese word for plain cooked rice. Also the word for meal.

Meal – *Shokuji* – A Japanese meal.

Meat – *Niku* – A general term for any kind of meat.

Minced fish – *Tataki* – A preparation method for fish, finely minced and seasoned with ginger, onion and *shiso*. Also refers to bonito or beef, lightly seared on the outside, sliced thin and served with ginger and soy sauce.

Mixed pickles – *Fukijinzuke* – A popular Japanese pickle medley, usually composed of seven vegetables, including *daikon*, eggplant, lotus root, ginger, *shiso* buds, turnip, *shitake* mushrooms, and other vegetables native to Japan.

Mixed Vegetables – *Aemono* – A mixture of cooked vegetables with a dressing or sauce.

Mollusk – *Kai* – A general term for any kind of mollusk, such as oysters, mussels, clams, etc.

Monkfish – *Anko* – A monkfish, native to the north Atlantic, also known as an anglerfish for the tendrils it uses for luring prey.

Monkfish liver – *Ankimo* – Monkfish liver, steamed or sautéed and dressed with vinegar.

Moray eel – *Utsubo* – A moray eel, a snake-like, carnivorous ocean fish.

Mountain vegetables – *Sansai* – A mixture of wild young mountain vegetables and greens indigenous to Japan. Served marinated or pickled.

MSG – *Ajinomoto* – A popular brand of MSG (monosodium glutamate).

Mugwort – *Yomogi* – A mugwort plant used in a variety of vegetable dishes.

Mung bean noodles – *Harusame* – Thin, transparent mung bean gelatin noodles, often used in *sunomono* appetizers.

Mushroom – *Enoki-take* – A tiny white mushroom that grows in bunches during the winter months.

Mushroom – *Mai-take* – Hen-of-the-wood, a Japanese mushroom used in many dishes.

Mushroom – *Matsutake* – A rare and expensive wild Japanese mushroom native to Japan and other northern climates, seasonal in autumn. One of Japan's most coveted delicacies.

Mushroom – *Nameko* – A golden-brown Japanese mushroom, usually available pickled or in cans, and often used in soups.

Mushroom – *Shiitake* – A Japanese mushroom, cultivated on the logs of the *shii* tree, a chestnut-oak, widely popular for a variety of Japanese dishes. Available fresh or dried.

Mushroom- *Shimeji* – A pale, delicate mushroom, also called *honshimeji*.

Mussel – *Igai* – A mussel, a freshwater bivalve mollusk, usually served steamed.

Mustard – *Karashi* – A hot Japanese mustard made from the seeds of several varieties of mustard plants.

Mustard soybean paste – *Karashi sumiso* – White *miso* seasoned with vinegar and *karashi* mustard, often served with *konnyaku*.

Needlefish – *Datsu* – A Pacific needlefish, also calle a sea pike, a predatory fish with a cylindrical body and elongated jaw, native to northern coastal waters. Commonly used to make *kamaboko* fish paste.

Oba – Perilla leaf, beefsteak plant, *shiso*.

Octopus – *Iidako* – A baby octopus, usually served boiled and marinated in a sweet soy sauce.

Octopus – *Tako* – An octopus, an eight tentacled cephalopod that turns a rosy purple when cooked. Usually served marinated, grilled or as *nigiri sushi*.

Octopus in vinegar – *Tako-su* – Octopus marinated in rice wine vinegar and mixed with fresh cucumber, served as a *sunomono* appetizer.

Omelet-wrapped sushi – *Fukusa-zushi* – *Sushi* wrapped with a thin omelet.

Onion- *Negi* – A scallion or spring onion, used as a simple garnish for soups and *sushi*, and in many other Japanese dishes.

Oregon roll – *Makizushi* roll filled with smoked salmon.

Original sushi – *Narezushi* – The original form of *sushi*, a fermenting process developed in ancient Asia as a means of preserving fish.

Osaka-style sushi – *Battera* – Osaka-style box *sushi*, with a layer of pressed rice topped with pickled mackerel and a paper-thin slice of *konbu* sea kelp. Also called *oshizushi*.

Osaka-style sushi – *Oshizushi* – Osaka-style *sushi*, boxes of pressed rice topped with thin slices of fish and cut into bite-sized pieces.

Oyster – *Kaki* – An oyster, a mollusk with a rough nacreous shell, native to coastal waters all over the world. Served on the half-shell in *sushi* bars, also popular fried.

Oyster Mushroom – *Hiratake* – Oyster mushroom.

Oysters in vinegar – *Sugaki* – Oysters marinated in vinegar. A *sunomono* appetizer, often served with *ponzu* dipping sauce.

Pair sushi – *Nigiri sushi* – Served in pairs, this style of *sushi* consists of slices of raw fish or pieces of other types of seafood, placed atop oblong balls of vinegared rice. Also called *Edo-mae sushi*, which literally means 'in front of Edo,' the name of old Tokyo.

Parrotfish – *Budai* – A parrotfish, a colorful tropical fish with a beak-like tooth formation.

Parrotfish – *Ishidai* – A parrotfish, a colorful tropical fish with a beak-like tooth formation.

Pear – *Nashi* – A Japanese pear.

Peponita – A red clam, a burrowing mollusk, also called *peponita*, cockle or ark shell, with tender, rosy flesh, often eaten raw.

Pepper – *Sansho* – Japanese pepper, the seeds of the prickly ash, ground into a powder and used by itself or in a blend with other spices.

Perch – *Fukko* – A young freshwater perch with spiny fins.

Perch – *Menuke* – A rockfish or ocean perch, a spawning fish with dark horizontal stripes, native to the rocky coastal northern waters.

Perilla – *Aojiso* – A *shiso* leaf, a perilla, also known as the beefsteak plant, a member of the mint family. Used as a garnish for *sushi* and *sashimi*, and also fried *tempura*-style.

Perilla bud – *Shisonomi* – A *shiso* bud, used as a garnish, or in salads or fried *tempura*-style.

Perilla leaf – *Shiso* – A perilla, or beefsteak plant, a piquant leaf, in both green and red varieties, widely used in Japanese cuisine as a garnish, flavoring agent, pickled, or fried *tempura*-style.

Philadelphia roll – *Makizushi* roll filled with salmon and cream cheese.

Pickle – *Suzuke* – A vinegar pickle, *tsukemono*.

Pickle rolls – *Oshinkomaki* – *Makizushi* rolls filled with Japanese pickles, especially *daikon* radish.

Pickle rolls – *Tsukemono maki* – *Makizushi* rolls filled with various Japanese pickles.

Pickled entrails – *Shiokara* – Salt-cured fish, shellfish and their entrails, with squid being the most popular.

Pickled fish – *Nanabanzuke* – Portuguese-style pickled fish.

Pickled ginger– *Gari* – Pickled ginger, thinly sliced and served as an accompaniment to *sushi*. Also called *gari shoga*.

Pickled radish – *Batterazuke* – *Daikon* radish pickled with *koji* fermenting starter.

Pickled radish – *Takuan zuke* – Pickled *daikon* radish, bright yellow, crunchy, commonly served as a side dish or as *shinko maki* rolls. Also called *Takuan-maki*, named for Takuan Soho, the Buddhist monk who is credited with its invention.

Pickled radish rolls – *Shinko maki* – *Makizushi* rolls filled with bright yellow pickled *daikon* radish. Also called *Takuan-maki*, named for Takuan Soho, the Buddhist monk who is credited with its invention.

Pickled sour plum – *Umeboshi* – A pickled sour plum, very salty and tart, used as a filling for *onigiri* rice balls, and as a flavoring agent for other Japanese dishes.

Pickled vegetables in soybean paste – *Moromi miso* – Vegetables pickled in *moromi* and *miso,* sometimes served on cucumber slices.

Pickles – *Hishio* – A category of Japanese pickled and fermented dishes that includes *tsukemono* and *shiokara*.

Pickles – *Ko no mono* – A general term for Japanese pickles, also called *tsukemono*.

Pickles – *Oshinko* – A general term for Japanese pickles.

Pickles – *Tsukemono* – A general term for Japanese pickles, of which there are a wide variety of regional styles, ingredients and preparation methods.

Pickles with soybean paste – *Misozuke* – Japanese pickles cured with *miso*.

Pink salmon – *Karafuto masu* – A type of pink salmon, especially valued for its roe.

Plaice – *Hoshi garei* – A spotted plaice, a large European flatfish.

Plaice – *Karei* – A halibut, plaice, flounder, or sand dab, a flatfish with a migrating eye, native to northern waters. Especially favored for *sashimi*.

Plaice – *Mako garei* – A plaice or flatfish, native to northern waters.

Polished white rice – *Hakumai* – Polished white rice.

Pollack – *Mentai* – An Alaskan Pollack or cod, rarely eaten raw, but valued for its roe.

Pollack – *Suketodara* – An Alaskan pollack, also called *mentai*, a codfish native to northern waters. Especially valued for its roe. Also spelled *sukesodara*.

Pollack roe – *Mentaiko* – The roe of the Alaskan pollack, often mixed with cayenne pepper and colored bright red, used as a garnish for some kinds of *sushi*. Also called *karashi-mentaiko*.

Pomfret – *Mana gatsuo* – A silver pomfret, a meaty, dark-skinned fish with spiny fins, native to northern waters.

Porgy – *Ishigakidai* – A rock porgy, a lean fish native to tropical coastal waters worldwide.

Potato – *Imo* – A Japanese word for potato, including yams, sweet potatoes, and taro root.

Powdered radish – *Kona wasabi* – Powdered *wasabi* root.

Powdered seasoning – *Furikake* – A condiment or topping blend of seaweed flakes, sesame seeds and dried fish powder.

Prepared foods – *Neri* – A Japanese prefix which means 'prepared,' often used to describe pastes or powdered seasonings.

Pressed sushi – *Battera* – Osaka-style box *sushi*, with a layer of pressed rice topped with pickled mackerel and a paper-thin slice of *konbu* sea kelp. Also called *oshizushi*.

Prickly ash – *Kinome* – Leaves of the Japanese prickly ash (*sansho*), used in soups and to flavor simmered foods.

Prickly ash – *Kinome* – Young leaves of the *sansho* tree, a prickly ash.

Pumpkin – *Kabocha* – A pumpkin or winter squash, widely used in a variety of dishes including *tempura*.

Purple laver – *Asakusanori* – Purple laver, the most common variety of algae, used to make sheets of toasted seaweed paper.

Quail egg – *Uzura-tamago* – A quail egg, often used as a topping on *gunkan maki*.

Radish – *Daikon* – A large, carrot-shaped white radish (*Raphanus sativus*), commonly used in Japanese cuisine. A *daikon* can weigh up to seven pounds and is often served pickled, or finely shredded as an attractive garnish for some Japanese dishes, especially *sashimi*.

Radish – *Suzushiro* – An old name for *daikon* radish.

Radish sprout – *Kaiware-* Daikon sprouts, peppery young shoots used as garnish or salad.

Radish sprout rolls – *Kaiware maki* – *Makizushi* rolls filled with peppery *daikon* radish sprouts.

Rainbow roll – *Makizushi* roll with thin slices of raw fish and avocado wrapped around the outside of a California roll. Also called *Geisha* roll, Caterpillar roll, and Dragon roll.

Rainbow trout – *Nijimasu* – A rainbow trout, a spawning fish native to the northern Pacific, widely cultivated at commercial farms in Japan. Served as *sashimi* or grilled.

Rainbowfish – *Bera* – A rainbowfish, native to the fresh waters of South America and the West Indies, commonly used to make *kamaboko* fish paste.

Rainbowfish – *Gizami* – A rainbowfish, native to the fresh waters of South America and West Indies, commonly used to make *kamaboko* fish paste. Also called *bera*.

Ramune – A popular Japanese brand of bottled lemonade that comes in a distinctive blue bottle sealed with a glass marble.

Rape buds – *Nanohana* – The immature buds of the rape plant, similar in appearance to broccoli, often served pickled.

Rape Plant – *Aburana* – The rape plant, used mostly for its oil, but its greens are also served as a vegetable.

Rape seed – *Natane* – The seeds of the rape plant, used for their oil. Also called canola oil.

Raw – *Nama* – A Japanese prefix that means fresh or raw. Used to describe foods and also draft beer.

Raw salad – *Namasu* – A dish of raw fish or meat mixed with vegetables and dressed with vinegar.

Razor shell clam – *Mategai* – A razor shell clam with a long narrow shell, named for its shape, which resembles a straight razor.

Razor-shell clam – *Tairagai* – A razor-shell clam, also called fan shell, pen shell or sea pen, valued for its adductor muscle, which is served as *sashimi* or *sunomono*.

Red beans – *Azuki* – Small, dark red beans used in a variety of Japanese dishes and pastries.

Red Beefsteak Plant – *Akajiso* – Red perilla, the leaves of the beefsteak plant, sometimes used as a coloring agent, especially for *umeboshi* (sour pickled plums).

Red Clam – *Akagai* – A red clam, a burrowing mollusk, also called *peponita*, cockle or ark shell, with tender, rosy flesh. Often eaten raw.

Red ginger – *Benishoga* – Red pickled ginger, colored with sour plum vinegar and red *shiso* leaf.

Red Miso Soup – *Akadashi* – *Miso* soup made with *akamiso*, a reddish soybean paste.

Red Perilla – *Akajiso* – Red perilla, the leaves of the beefsteak plant, sometimes used as a coloring agent, especially for *umeboshi* (sour pickled plums).

Red Rockfish – *Akodai* – A red rockfish with silvery skin and horizontal stripes, native to the rocky northern coastlines of Europe and North America.

Red sea bream – *Madai* – A red snapper or red sea bream, any of several large sharp-toothed fish, native to tropical coastal waters.

Red sea bream with cod roe – *Madai tarako-ae* – Red Sea Bream served with cod roe.

Red snapper – *Madai* – A red snapper or red sea bream, any of several large sharp-toothed fish, native to tropical coastal waters.

Rice – *Gohan* – Cooked rice. Also a Japanese word for 'meal.'

Rice – *Kome* – A Japanese term for uncooked rice.

Rice – *Meshi* – Cooked rice. Also a Japanese word for 'meal.'

Rice – *Shari* – Another word for *sushi* rice.

Rice balls – *Onigiri* – Balls of sticky rice, either plain or filled with various ingredients, often wrapped in *nori* seaweed paper. A popular treat for Japanese lunchboxes.

Rice dumplings – *Mochi* – Japanese rice dumplings made by pounding glutinous rice into a rubbery dough. Prepared in many ways from grilled skewers to sweet cakes.

Rice liquor – *Shochu* – A strong, distilled spirit made from rice or potatoes.

Rice wine – *Ikkyu* – A premium grade of *sake*.

Rice wine – *Nihon shu* – Japanese rice wine, *sake*.

Rice wine – *Nikyu* – A lesser grade of *sake*.

Rice wine – *Sake* – Japanese rice wine, available in many styles and grades of quality.

Rice wine – *Tokkyu* – A premium-grade *sake*, usually served only on special occasions.

Rice wine lees – *Kasu* – The lees or dregs of the *sake* fermentation process, sometimes used in soups and pickles.

River crab – *Sawagani* – A river crab, tiny freshwater crab native to Japan. Usually deep-fried and served whole as a crunchy snack.

Rock cod – *Mebaru* – A rock cod, a lean white fish native to the north Atlantic.

Rock Trout – *Ainame* – A freshwater rock trout or greenling, sometimes served as *sashimi*.

Rockfish – *Kasago* – A marbled rockfish, a spawning fish with dark horizontal stripes, native to the rocky coastal waters of Europe and North America.

Rockfish – *Menuke* – A rockfish or ocean perch, a spawning fish with dark horizontal stripes, native to the rocky coastal northern waters.

Royal fern – *Zenmai* – A royal fern or fiddlehead fern used in many Japanese dishes.

Sablefish – *Gindara* – A sablefish, native to the Bering Sea. Usually served cooked.

Sailfin – *Hata-hata* – A sailfin or sandfish, two types of small silver scaleless burrowing fish, native to the north Pacific.

Salad – *Sarada* – The Japanese pronunciation of 'salad,' which may mean any of a number of types of fresh green dishes. Also called *nama yasai*.

Salad with vinegar dressing – *Sunomono* – A salad dressed with vinegar. Its name literally means 'vinegared things' and may include a wide variety of vegetables and bits of minced seafood. Often served as a complimentary appetizer at *sushi* bars.

Salmon – *Sake* – A salmon, any of several varieties of spawning fish, native to cool northern waters. Susceptible to parasites in the wild, so most *sushi* grade salmon is farm raised or must be treated by freezing, salting, marinating or smoking.

Salmon roe – *Ikura* – Salmon roe, large, bright orange fish eggs filled with salty juice, often served as *gunkan-maki* or as a delicate garnish on other types of *sushi*.

Salmon roe in the sac – *Sujiko* – Salmon roe in the sac, preserved with salt or pickled with *sake*.

Salmon skin rolls – *Sakekawa maki* – *Makizushi* rolls or *temaki* rolls filled with broiled salmon skin.

Salt – *Morijio* – A small pile of salt, a Japanese purification ritual and offering to the gods for their protection. Small piles of salt can be seen at the entrances of many shrines and businesses in Japan. Salt is also placed at the entrances of bars and restaurants to attract customers.

Salt – *Shio* – The Japanese word for salt.

Salt grilling – *Shioyaki* – A general term for salt-grilling.

Salt pickle – *Shiozuke* – A general term for a salt pickle, the most common method of pickling vegetables.

Salt pickles – *Nazuke* – Japanese salt pickles, made with a variety of leafy vegetables, often served as *tsukemono*.

Saltwater Eel – *Anago* – A conger eel, a dark, snake-like ocean fish native to tropical coastal waters, always served cooked.

Saltwater Eel rolls – *Anakyu* – *Makizushi* rolls filled with saltwater eel (*anago*).

Salty-sweet salad – *Tsukudani* – A salty-sweet mixture of seafood, vegetables or both, seasoned with soy sauce and *mirin*.

Sand dab – *Karei* – A halibut, plaice, flounder, or sand dab, a flatfish with a migrating eye, native to northern waters. Especially favored for *sashimi*.

Sandfish – *Hata-hata* – A sailfin or sandfish, two types of small silver scaleless burrowing fish, native to the north Pacific.

Sardine – *Iwashi* – A sardine or herring, small fish that swims in large schools, native to the coastal waters in many parts of the world. Sometimes served as *sashimi* or grilled. Usually available canned.

Sardine – *Shirasu* – A young sardine, usually boiled, dried and used for simmered broths.

Sauce – *Tare* – A general term for any kind of thick sauce, usually made with sweetened soy sauce or *miso*.

Sauces – *Nitsume* – A general term for condensed sauces.

Sawedged perch – *Ara* – A sawedged perch with spiny fins, a freshwater fish native to Europe and North America.

Scallion pickle – *Rakkyo* – Pickled scallion.

Scallop – *Hotategai* – A giant sea scallop, a fan-shaped mollusk with, mild, sweet, delicate white flesh. Its roe is also considered a delicacy.

Scallop adductor muscle – *Hotategai kaibashira* – The adductor muscle of a sea scallop, considered a delicacy.

Scattered sushi – *Barazushi* – A bowl of vinegared rice topped with slices of raw fish and other *sushi* ingredients. Also called *chirashizushi* (scattered *sushi*), or *gomokuzushi* (five-item *sushi*).

Scattered sushi – *Chirashizushi* – A bowl of vinegared rice with slices of raw fish and other *sushi* toppings. Its name means 'scattered *sushi*.' Also known as *barazushi*, or *gomokuzushi* (five-item *sushi*).

Scattered sushi – *Gomokuzushi* – A bowl of vinegared rice with slices of raw fish and other *sushi* toppings. Its name means 'five item *sushi*.' Also known as *chirashizushi* or *barazushi*.

Sea bass – *Seigo* – A young sea bass with a long body and spiny fins, native to the north Atlantic.

Sea bass – *Suzuki* – A sea bass, a large, firm white-fleshed fish, often served as *sashimi* or *sushi*.

Sea bream – *Kasugo* – A young sea bream.

Sea bream – *Tai* – A sea bream native to the sea surrounding Japan, highly valued for its delicate, translucent flesh, usually served very thinly sliced. Because its name also means 'congratulations,' it is a popular choice for celebratory meals. The word *tai* is also used to refer to red snapper or porgy.

Sea cucumber – *Namako* – A sea cucumber or sea slug, named for its cucumber-shaped body, tough and crunchy, served raw in Japan.

Sea grass – *Hama bofu* – A seaside plant, often served with *sashimi*, or as a garnish for vinegared fish *sunomono*.

Sea pike – *Datsu* – A Pacific needlefish, also called a sea pike, a predatory fish with a cylindrical body and elongated jaw, native to northern coastal waters. Commonly used to make *kamaboko* fish paste.

Sea slug – *Namako* – A sea cucumber or sea slug, named for its cucumber-shaped body, tough and crunchy, served raw in Japan.

Sea slug entrails – *Konowata* – Fermented sea slug entrails, one of Japan's three most prized delicacies.

Sea snail – *Bai* – A small sea snail, or whelk, used for making vinegared *sunomono* appetizers.

Sea snail – *Sazae* – A sea snail, also called turban shell or turbo, usually served steamed in the shell or sliced and marinated.

Sea snail – *Tsubu* – A Japanese sea snail native to Hokkaido.

Sea squirt – *Hoya* – A sea squirt, a tiny, sedentary invertebrate with a sac-like body with siphons that can contract to eject streams of water to escape predators. Their flesh is eaten raw, and their intestines are mixed with vinegar to make *sunomono*, or fermented to make *shiokara*.

Sea urchin glands – *Uni* – The reproductive glands of a sea urchin, a mustard-colored shellfish with a strong flavor, usually served as *gunkan-maki*, an expensive seasonal delicacy.

Seafood – *Gyokairui* – A general term for seafood.

Season – *Shun* – The peak season for any kind of seafood, vegetable or fruit.

Seasoned nori – *Ajitsuke nori* – Seasoned *nori*.

Seasoned Salt – *Ajishio* – Seasoned salt, usually with MSG.

Seasoning – *Chomiryo* – The Japanese word for 'seasoning' or 'condiment.'

Seasoning – *Ajitsuke* – A general term for a seasoning or flavoring agent.

Seaweed – *Kaiso* – A general term for seaweed.

Seaweed – *Wakame* – A delicate seaweed, most commonly available dried, used in a variety of dishes such as *miso* soup and *sunomono*.

Seaweed noodles – *Tokoroten* – Thin, gelatinous seaweed noodles mixed with soy sauce and vinegar, served cold as an appetizer.

Seaweed paper – *Nori* – An edible seaweed paper made from a variety of algae called *Porphyra*, also called laver. Once it has been harvested from the sea, the algae is pulverized and laid out in thin sheets to dry. It is then cut into uniform squares and packaged for commercial distribution. *Nori* is commonly used as a wrap for *sushi* and *onigiri*, as well as a shredded topping for soups, rice and noodles.

Seaweed paper – *Suizenji nori* – A rare form of blue-green algae used to make *nori* sheets or preserved in brine for an accompaniment to *sashimi* or in *sunomono* or soup.

Seaweed rolls – *Isobe* – A general term for anything wrapped in or garnished with *nori*.

Seaweed rolls – *Makizushi* – This variety of *sushi* is composed of vinegared rice and bits of fish or seafood, wrapped cigar-style in a sheet of toasted seaweed paper called *nori*, and sliced into six bite-sized pieces.

Seaweed rolls – *Norimaki* – *Sushi* rolled in sheets of *nori* seaweed paper with vinegared rice and various fillings.

Seaweed rolls – *Sushi maki* – A variety of *sushi* composed of vinegared rice and bits of fish or seafood, wrapped cigar-style in a sheet of toasted seaweed paper called *nori*, and sliced into bite-sized pieces. Also called *makizushi*.

Semi-fatty tuna – *Chu-toro* – The semi-fatty cut of *maguro*, taken from the lower broad side of the tuna.

Sesame salt – *Goma shio* – Sesame salt, a blend of salt and ground sesame seeds, commonly found on Japanese tables.

Sesame seeds – *Goma* – Sesame seeds, widely used as a garnish for *makizushi*.

Sesame seeds – *Irigoma* – Toasted sesame seeds.

Sesame seeds – *Shiro goma* – White sesame seeds.

Set meal – *Teishoku* – A Japanese set meal, several items for a fixed price.

Seven spice powder – *Nanairo togarashi* – A spice blend with seven ingredients, including red pepper (*togarashi*), ground *sansho* pepper pods, dried mandarin orange peel, black hemp seeds or white poppy seeds, *nori* seaweed bits, and white sesame seeds. Also called *shichimi togarashi*.

Seven spice powder – *Shichimi togarashi* – A blend of seven spices, including red pepper (*togarashi*), ground *sansho*, pepper pods, dried mandarin orange peel, black hemp seeds or white poppy seeds, *nori* seaweed bits, and white sesame seeds.

Seville orange – *Daidai*- A bitter Japanese citrus fruit, also called Seville orange. Its juice is mixed with soy sauce to make *ponzu*.

Sevruga caviar – *Seburuga* – The Japanese pronunciation of Sevruga caviar.

Shaddock – *Zabon* – A shaddock or pomelo.

Shark – *Fuka* – A large carnivorous shark with tough skin and rugged scales.

Shark – *Same* – A shark, never served raw for *sushi*, but sometimes served marinated as *sunomono*.

Shark skin – *Samegawa* – The skin of a shark.

Shellfish – A general term for any kind of mollusk, such as oysters, mussels, clams, etc.

Shiner – *Moroko* – A willow shiner, a small, silvery fish native to the North Atlantic and Mediterranean Sea.

Short-necked clam – *Asari* – A short-necked clam, always served cooked, sometimes in vinegared appetizers called *sunomono*.

Shredded ingredients – *Sengiri* – A general term for any kind of shredded ingredient, such as cabbage or *daikon* radish.

Shredded radish – *Daikon-oroshi* – Finely shredded *daikon* radish, usually served as a garnish for *sashimi* and other *sushi*.

Shrimp – *Ebi* – A shrimp, any of a wide variety of species. Usually refers to the cooked variety served as *nigiri sushi*.

Shrimp – *Taisho ebi* – A plump, fleshy shrimp.

Shrimp heads – *Ebi no atama* – Shrimp heads, served deep-fried as a side dish with an order of *amaebi*, raw sweet shrimp.

Side dish – *Sozai* – A general term for a side dish of any kind. Also called *osozai* or *okazu*.

Silver fish – *Hikarimono* – A general term for any variety of silver fish, its name literally means 'shiny things.' Also, fish sliced for serving with the silver skin left intact, especially *aji*, *sanma*, and *kohada*.

Skipjack – *Katsuo* – A skipjack or bonito, an ocean-going variety of smaller tuna, native to both Atlantic and Pacific waters.

Skipjack slices – *Katsuo no tataki* – Dark, young skipjack *sashimi*, richly flavored, aged and seared, served with ginger and green onion.

Smelt – *Shishamo* – A smelt, a small, silver ocean or freshwater fish native to cold northern waters. Often served grilled whole with roe intact.

Smelt – *Wakasagi* – A pond smelt, a small silvery fish that migrates between fresh and salt water. Often served in vinegar or deep-fried *tempura* style.

Smelt roe – *Masago* – Smelt roe, tiny orange fish eggs, finer but similar in appearance to flying fish roe.

Smoked bonito – *Namaribushi* – Partially smoked bonito, sometimes served as an appetizer with mixed vegetables.

Snack foods – *Tsumamimono* – Snack foods served with alcoholic beverages.

Snapper – *Tai* – A sea bream native to the sea surrounding Japan, highly valued for its delicate, translucent flesh, usually served very thinly sliced. Because its name also means 'congratulations,' it is a popular choice for celebratory meals. The word *tai* is also used to refer to red snapper or porgy.

Snow crab – *Matsubagani* – a Matsuba crab or Pacific snow crab. Also called *zuwaigani* in eastern Japan.

Snow crab – *Zuwaigani* – A snow crab native to the Sea of Japan, served as *sashimi*, *sunomono* and *tempura*.

Snow pea – *Sayaendo* – A snow pea or sugar pea.

Sockeye salmon – *Benizake* – A small sockeye salmon native to rivers and tributaries of the north Pacific.

Sole – *Shita birame* – A sole, a flatfish with a migrating eye, native to warm waters.

Soup – *Shiru* – A general term for any kind of soup or sauce.

Soup stock – *Dashi* – An all-purpose stock for soups and simmered dishes usually made with *kombu* (a type of sea kelp) and flavored with dried *shiitake* or *katsuoboshi* (bonito flakes).

Sour plum liquor – *Umeshu* – A strong spirit flavored with pickled sour plum.

Sour plum with perilla – *Ume shiso* – A mixture of plum paste and *shiso* leaf, sometimes used as a filling for *makizushi*. Also called *umejiso*.

Soy sauce – *Murasaki* – A *sushi* bar term for soy sauce, the word means 'purple.'

Soy sauce – *Shoyu* – Fermented soy sauce made with soybeans, wheat and salt, an essential component of every Japanese meal.

Soy sauce – *Tamari* – Soy sauce brewed without wheat.

Soy sauce boiled – *Nikiri* – Soy sauce that has been boiled.

Soy sauce with vinegar – *Nihaizu* – A mixture of vinegar and soy sauce, sometimes diluted with *dashi*.

Soybean curd – *Katadofu* – A firm, coarse textured *tofu*.

Soybean curd – *Momendofu* – A Japanese name for the common variety of *tofu*.

Soybean curd – *Tofu* – Soybean curd, made by boiling ground soybeans with water, and then shaped into blocks. Available in many styles and textures, and used in a wide variety of Japanese dishes, or it may be eaten by itself with various sauces and toppings.

Soybean curd dressing – *Shira ae* – A cooked salad mixed in a *tofu* dressing.

Soybean paste – *Miso* – A fermented soybean paste, sometimes mixed with fermented barley or rice. Available in many colors and styles, used to make pickles, sauces, marinades and most importantly, *miso shiru*, a classic Japanese broth served with nearly every Japanese meal.

Soybean paste soup – *Miso shiru* – Japan's most popular soup, a broth made with a sea kelp and dried bonito broth called *dashi*, mixed with *miso* paste and garnished with cubes of *tofu* and bits of seaweed or other vegetables.

Soybean – *Sayamame* – A soybean. Also called *edamame*.

Soybeans in the pod – *Edamame* – A type of young green soybean, boiled in the pods. This summer treat is a popular *sushi* bar appetizer, or a complimentary snack food served alongside cold draft beers in Japanese *izakaya* pubs, where patrons pop open the pods much like salted peanuts, and munch on the tasty beans within. Also called *sayamame*.

Spanish mackerel – *Sawara* – A Spanish mackerel native to the north Atlantic and Gulf of Mexico as well as to Japan's Inland Sea. Since it is a spawning fish, it is not suitable for *sashimi* due to freshwater parasites.

Spanish mackerel sashimi – *Aji no tataki* – Spanish mackerel *sashimi*, sliced from a small mackerel and served in the hollowed-out remains of its own carcass.

Spice – *Koshinryo* – A general term for spices, including hemp seeds, sesame seeds, mustard, poppy seeds, prickly ash seeds, ginger, chili pepper, *wasabi* and citron.

Spider roll – *Makizushi* roll filled with softshell crab *tempura*.

Spinach – *Horenso* – Spinach, which is used in many different Japanese dishes.

Sponge cake – *Taiyaki* – A sponge cake molded in the shape of a sea bream, served at children's celebrations.

Spring salmon – *Sakura masu* – A salmon trout, its name means 'cherry-blossom trout.'

Spring sea bream – *Sakura-dai* – A spring red sea bream, its name means 'cherry-blossom bream.'

Spring shrimp – *Sakura ebi* – A type of shrimp, its name means 'cherry blossom shrimp.'

Squid – *Ika* – A squid, a cuttlefish, a tubular translucent, tentacled cephalopod, usually served thinly sliced with *shiso* leaf.

Squid – *Yari ika* – A long-finned squid.

Squid entrails – *Ika no shiokara* – Fermented squid entrails, salty and pale pink in color.

Squid in soy sauce – *Ni ika* – Squid simmered in soy sauce.

Squid noodles – *Ika somen* – Squid 'noodles,' thinly sliced raw squid mixed with quail egg, *wasabi*, and seaweed.

Squid salad – *Ika sansai* – Marinated squid with mountain vegetables.

Squid tentacles – *Geso* – Squid tentacles, often prepared with *teriyaki* sauce.

Squid tentacles – *Ika-geso* – Squid tentacles, often prepared with *teriyaki* sauce.

Squid thinly sliced – *Ika no sengiri* – Very thinly sliced squid, its name means 'a thousand slices.'

Squid with fermented soybeans – *Ika natto* – Thinly sliced squid mixed with fermented soybeans. Sometimes used as a filling for *makizushi* or *temaki*.

Squid with spicy cod roe – *Ika mentai* – Squid with spicy *mentaiko* cod roe, served as *sashimi* or used to fill *makizushi* or *temaki* hand rolls.

Steamed foods – *Mushimono* – A general term for steamed foods.

Stingfish – *Okoze* – A stingfish, also called stonefish or scorpion fish. A venomous tropical fish with rock-like camouflage.

Stonefish – *Okoze* – A stingfish, also called stonefish or scorpion fish. A venomous tropical fish with rock-like camouflage.

Striped – *Shima* – A prefix meaning 'striped,' usually referring to fish such as *shima aji*.

Strong seasonings – *Yakumi* – Any kind of strongly flavored seasoning, such as *shichimi togarashi*, grated *daikon*, or spring onion.

Sturgeon – *Chosame* – A sturgeon, native to northern waters, especially valued for its caviar, but its flesh is never eaten raw. Its Japanese name means 'butterfly shark.'

Sugar – *Sato* – The Japanese word for sugar.

Sunfish – *Manbo* – An ocean sunfish in the perch family, with a compact, oval body, native to warm waters.

Surf clam – *Aoyagi* – A surf clam or round clam, often eaten raw but turns brilliant red when steamed.

Surf clam – *Hokki gai* – A red-tipped surf clam, also called hen clam, off-white when served as *sashimi* and *sushi*, but turns bright pink when cooked.

Surf clam – *Kobashira* – A surf clam.

S**ushi pie**ce – *Kan* – A counting unit for *nigiri sushi*, one piece.

Sweet Shrimp – *Amaebi* – A sweet translucent shrimp, native to cold northern waters, usually served raw with its head and tentacles served deep-fried.

Sweetfish – *Ayu* – A small, sweet freshwater fish, native to the rivers of Japan, caught using trained cormorant birds. Usually served grilled.

Sweetfish entrails – *Uruka* – Sweetfish entrails prepared as *shiodara*.

Swordfish – *Kajiki* – A swordfish, a large, toothless fish with a long sword-like snout, native to the ocean floor of warm waters. Often eaten as *sashimi* or *sushi*.

Swordfish – *Mekajiki* – A swordfish, a large, toothless fish with a long sword-like snout, native to the ocean floor of warm waters.

Tangerine – *Mikan* – A mandarin orange or tangerine.

Taro root – *Sato imo* – Taro root.

Tea – *Cha* – The Japanese word for tea, available in many types and grades of quality. Also called *ocha*.

Tea – *Gyokuro* – Japan's rarest, most expensive tea, *gyokuro* is made from the tender first tea leaves of spring.

Tempura shrimp rolls – *Ebi Tempura maki* – *Makizushi* rolls filled with *tempura* shrimp.

Thinly sliced fish – *Usu-zukuri* – A method of preparing *sashimi*, especially *fugu* and *hirame*, in which paper-thin slices of translucent white fish are decoratively arranged on a plate.

Thinly sliced ingredients – *Usugiri* – A general term for thinly sliced ingredients.

Thin–sliced halibut – *Hirame Usuzukuri* – A method of preparing halibut *sashimi* in very thin, translucent slices, served with *ponzu* sauce.

Tiger prawn – *Kuruma ebi* – A tiger prawn.

Tilapia – *Izumidai* – A tilapia fish, similar in appearance to snapper or *tai*, with firm translucent flesh and red stripes.

Tilefish – *Amadai* – A tilefish native to western Japan.

Tiny Mushrooms – *Enoki-take* – A tiny white mushroom that grows in bunches during the winter months.

Tiny Shrimp – *Ami* – A tiny variety of shrimp, often made into pickled appetizers such as *shiokara*.

Toasted seaweed paper – *Yakinori* – Toasted seaweed paper.

Tofu sushi – *Inarizushi* – Pouches of deep-fried *tofu* filled with vinegared rice and other ingredients, such as pickles and sour plums.

Tokyo-style sushi – *Edomaezushi* – Tokyo-style *nigiri sushi*. Its name means 'in front of Tokyo.'

Trefoil – *Mitsuba* – A trefoil plant, similar in flavor to chervil and widely used in Japanese cooking .

Trout – *Iwana* – A char, any of several small-scaled trout, native to cold streams.

Trout – *Kawamasu* – A brook trout or char, originally from North America and introduced to Japan. Usually served cooked.

Trout – *Masu* – A trout, any of a variety of freshwater fish, commonly cultivated in commercial hatcheries. Usually served in specialty restaurants.

Tuna – *Maguro* – Any of several varieties of tuna, an ocean-going fish most popular for *sashimi* and *nigiri sushi*.

Tuna – *Meji Maguro* – A young tuna.

Tuna and cucumber rolls – *Tekkappa maki* – A combination of both tuna and cucumber rolls.

Tuna and onion rolls – *Negi-toro maki* – *Makizushi* rolls filled with raw tuna and spring onion.

Tuna and yam rolls – *Yama-kake maki* – *Makizushi* rolls filled with raw tuna and mountain potato.

Tuna for sushi rolls – *Tekka* – A *sushi* term for tuna, especially when used as a filling for *makizushi*.

Tuna hand roll – *Maguro temaki* – *Temaki* hand roll filled with raw tuna.

Tuna in soybean paste – *Maguro sai-kyo yaki* – Seared tuna marinated in *miso*.

Tuna over rice – *Tekka don* – Thin slices of raw tuna over rice.

Tuna rolls – *Tekka maki* – *Makizushi* rolls filled with raw tuna. Much like the origin of the sandwich, *tekkamaki* was Japan's first 'fast food,' prepared for gamblers in dice casinos called *tekkaba*, so that they could eat with one hand and roll dice with the other. And thus the tasty treat called *tekkamaki* got its name.

Tuna with onion – *Negi toro* – Raw tuna mixed with green onion.

Tuna with seaweed – *Maguro nyuta* – Raw tuna mixed with *wakame* seaweed and green onion topped with *miso*.

Tuna with soy sauce – *Zuke* – Raw tuna dipped in soy sauce.

Tuna with yam – *Yamakake* – Raw tuna mixed with mountain potato, *wasabi*, quail egg, and seaweed.

Turban shell – *Bateira* – A turban shell, a conical shellfish, often served as a vinegared *sunomono* appetizer.

Turnip – *Kabura* – A Japanese turnip, widely used in pickles as well as other dishes.

Turnip – *Sugukina* – A Japanese turnip, often served pickled, especially Kyoto-style.

Turnip – *Suzuna* – A Japanese turnip, often used in pickles and other vegetable dishes.

Turnip greens – *Nozawana* – Turnip greens, often used in pickles and *tsukemono*.

Turtle – *Suppon* – A soft-shelled snapping turtle indigenous to Japan, served as *sashimi* or deep-fried. Also used to make soup stock.

Twig tea – *Kukicha* – A tea made from roasted tea twigs and stems.

Unfiltered liquid – *Moromi* – A Japanese term for unfiltered liquids such as *sake, mirin,* and soy sauce. A fermenting slurry that forms during the brewing process just before filtration.

Vegetable rolls – *Yasai maki* – *Makizushi* rolls filled with vegetables such as carrots, cucumber, mountain potato, burdock root, etc.

Vegetable salad – *Ohitashi* – Par-cooked vegetables seasoned with soy sauce and *mirin,* served chilled.

Vegetable shoots – *Mabikina* – Tender shoots of green vegetables, often used as garnishes or as *sushi* ingredients.

Vegetables – *Yasai* – A general term for cultivated vegetables.

Vegetables in soybean paste – *Nuta* – A mixture of fish and vegetables dressed with *miso* and vinegar.

Vinegar – *Su* – A general term for unseasoned rice vinegar.

Vinegared rice dishes – *Sushi* – Any of a large number of Japanese seafoods, vegetables and various other ingredients prepared in combination with vinegared rice.

Water pepper – *Benitade* – A water pepper with spicy purple leaves, sometimes served as an accompaniment for *sashimi.*

Water pepper – *Tade* – A Japanese water pepper, both green and red, used as a flavor enhancer for fish, and also as an ingredient in dipping sauces. The red variety is also a strong coloring agent, especially for pickled red ginger and sour plums.

Whale – *Kujira* – Whale meat, illegal in the U.S. but a popular delicacy in Japan.

White fish – *Shiromi* – Any of a number of white-fleshed fish, including *tai, hirame,* etc.

White radish – *Daikon* – A large, carrot-shaped white radish (*Raphanus sativus*), commonly used in Japanese cuisine. A *daikon* can weigh up to seven pounds and is often served pickled, or finely shredded as an attractive garnish for some Japanese dishes, especially *sashimi*.

White shrimp – *Shiba ebi* – A white shrimp.

White soybean paste dressing – *Sumiso* – White *miso* mixed with rice vinegar, a dressing commonly used for freshwater fish. Also called *koromo*.

Whitebait – *Shira-uo* – A whitebait, a young herring, sprat, or smelt, usually cooked whole and used in many different dishes.

Whiting – *Kisu* – A silver whiting, a cod-like fish served in many different ways.

Winter squash – *Kabocha* – A pumpkin or winter squash, widely used in a variety of dishes including *tempura*.

Worchestershire sauce – *Sosu* – A Japanese term for Worchestershire sauce. Also called *usuta sosu*.

Yam – *Yama-imo* – A Japanese yam or mountain potato. Also called *taro*, used to make Hawaiian poi, as well as a variety of traditional Japanese dishes.

Yam with sour plum – *Yama-imo ume* – Mountain potato topped with sour plum paste, sometimes used as a filling in *makizushi* or *temaki* rolls.

Yellow horse mackerel – *Ma aji* – A yellow horse mackerel. The prefix 'ma' means 'true.'

Yellowfin tuna – *Kihada* – A yellowfin tuna, up to 400 lbs. (181 kg.), native to tropical waters, served as *sashimi* and *sushi*.

Yellowjack – *Shima aji* – A striped yellowjack or mackerel with red striped white flesh, native to the western Atlantic and Gulf of Mexico.

Yellowtail – *Hamachi* – A young yellowtail with a distinctive yellow stripe along its sides and tail, native to the tropical waters of the Atlantic and Caribbean.

Yellowtail – *Inada* – A very young yellowtail.

Yellowtail – *Kimachi* – A small fish in the yellowtail family.

Yellowtail – *Warasa* – The youngest yellowtail.

Yellowtail shoulder – *Hamachi kama* – Yellowtail shoulder, a small, delicate piece of fish just behind the head. Usually served grilled.

sabi

About the Author:

With her lifelong love of Japan, its people and its culture, Celeste Heiter believes that she may have been Japanese in a previous incarnation. In this lifetime, however, Celeste was born in Mobile, Alabama, where she earned a Bachelor's degree in Art and English from the University of South Alabama. Inspired by a lifelong dream to visit the Great Buddha at Kamakura, she moved to Tokyo in 1988, where she spent two years teaching English conversation. Celeste now makes her home in California's beautiful Napa Valley, with the most treasured souvenir of her life in Japan: her son Will, who was born during her stay in Tokyo.

Celeste is the author of *Vignettes of Japan*, *Ganbatte Means Go For It*, and *Five Seven Five*.

Please visit Chopstick Cinema, Celeste's daily blog about her adventures in Asian food and film.
www.chopstickcinema.com

About the Photographer:

Marc Schultz is a Bangkok-based commercial and fine-art travel photographer. Commercially, Marc focuses mainly on corporate, advertising, lifestyle, product, food, and interior photography.

In 2002 Marc was elected to be an Associate (ARPS) of the Royal Photographic Society of England, one of the world's oldest and most prestigious professional photographic associations, for his work in the field of Visual Arts.

Marc has held workshops and given a number of talks on photography. Recently he taught two semesters of photography at the School of Architecture and Industrial Design, a new campus of King Mongkut's University of Technology in Thonburi, Bangkok.

Please visit Marc's Web site.
www.lightworxstudio.com

Khun Suvisuth Chantaraprateep ("Pu")
Food Stylist

With his expertise in design and styling, Suvisuth Chantaraprateep has gained prominence in the worlds of both Thai fashion and fine cuisine. Throughout his career, Pu has been active in styling for local agencies and photographers on fashion shoots, food ads, and magazine editorial layouts. Most recently he has been collaborating on a number of projects with Bangkok-based photographer Marc Schultz.

Nongyao Hook, ("Max")
Make-up Artist

Noted for her artistry and professionalism, Max Hook is a Thailand-based makeup artist who has perfected the skills she developed at the Westmore Academy of Cosmetic Arts in Hollywood. Her web address is www.maxhookmakeupartist.com.

Nanthacha Samrong, ("Timmy")
Make-up Artist

Makeup artist Timmy is affiliated with many of the major advertising agencies and is best known for his work in television commercials shot in Thailand.

Prapatsorn Guntira, ("Mint")
Model
Mint's modelling credits include being on the cover of the 2004 Girls of Asia Swimsuit Calendar which was distributed worldwide. Her photo appears on page 118.

Zilola Mirzarasulova
Model
Zilola, pictured on page 106, is originally from Uzbekistan. She is a young and upcoming model whose work is already well known throughout Asia.

Photo Research
Photo research for the chapter on Famous Sushi Bars was conducted by Pupak Navabpour.

Chef Akihiro Izumi
Tsu
Before his appointment as head chef of
Tsu, Akihiro Izumi's reputation in the art
of classical Japanese cuisine was established
at fine restaurants in Tokyo, New York,
California, and Hong Kong. Located in
the JW Marriott Bangkok, Tsu presents a
formal, elegant setting for Chef Aki's
award winning traditional cuisine.

Chef Hiroshi Kagata
Drinking Tea Eating Rice
Chef Hiroshi Kagata from Osaka brings his
extensive background in traditional Japanese
culinary skills to The Conrad Hotel's
Drinking Tea Eating Rice restaurant. A
specialist in *sashimi*, *sushi* and seafood
dishes, Chef Hiroshi is licensed in blowfish
preparation and an expert in "Kaiseki"
arrangement. (One of the chef's *sushi*
creations is pictured on the cover.)

Dave Lombardi

Wasabi

Dave Lombardi modeled Wasabi on the intimate *sushi* bars he enjoyed in Japan. His award winning restaurant was founded on the principle that only the best rice, freshest imported fish, and premium *sakes* would be served. Despite the addition of modern fusion items, the focus of Wasabi remains on traditional *sushi* and *sashimi*. Contact Dave at eat@wasabibangkok.com.

Nicholas Bovine

Koi

After gaining celebrity fame at the Los Angeles and New York locations, Bangkok's Koi Restaurant has quickly gained popularity for its California-accented Japanese cuisine. "The menu is constantly updated and perfected," notes executive chef Nicholas Bovine. "At Koi, diners can taste the flavor of each fresh ingredient. Different flavors should not overpower each other."

THINGSASIAN PRESS

Experience Asia Through the Eyes of Travelers

"To know the road ahead, ask those coming back."
(CHINESE PROVERB)

East meets West at ThingsAsian Press, where the secrets of Asia are revealed by the travelers who know them best. Writers who have lived and worked in Asia. Writers with stories to tell about basking on the beaches of Thailand, teaching English conversation in the exclusive salons of Tokyo, trekking in Bhutan, haggling with antique vendors in the back alleys of Shanghai, eating spicy noodles on the streets of Jakarta, photographing the children of Nepal, cycling the length of Vietnam's Highway One, traveling through Laos on the mighty Mekong, and falling in love on the island of Kyushu.

Inspired by the many expert, adventurous and independent contributors who helped us build **ThingsAsian.com**, our publications are intended for both active travelers and those who journey vicariously, on the wings of words.

ThingsAsian Press specializes in travel stories, photo journals, cultural anthologies, destination guides and children's books. We are dedicated to assisting readers explore the cultures of Asia through the eyes of experienced travelers.

www.thingsasianpress.com

TO ASIA WITH LOVE
A Connoisseurs' Guide to Cambodia, Laos, Thailand & Vietnam
Edited & with contributions by Kim Fay;
Photography by Julie Fay
5 1/2 x 8 1/2 inches; 248 pages;
paperback; color & b/w images
ISBN 0-9715940-3-1
US$18.00

STROLLING IN MACAU NEW!
A Visitor's Guide to Macau, Taipa, and Coloane
By Steven K. Bailey;
Photography by Jill C. Witt
5 1/2 x 8 1/2 inches; 208 pages;
paperback; color images; maps
ISBN-10: 0-9715940-9-0
ISBN-13: 978-0-9715940-9-8
US$14.95

VIGNETTES OF JAPAN
Fifty vignettes of an American's life in Japan
By Celeste Heiter;
Photography by Robert George
5 1/2 x 8 1/2 inches; 180 pages;
paperback; color images
ISBN 0-9715940-2-3
US$12.95

VIGNETTES OF TAIWAN
Short Stories, Essays & Random Meditations About Taiwan
By Joshua Samuel Brown;
5 1/2 x 8 1/2 inches; 160 pages;
paperback; color images
ISBN 0-9715940-8-2
US$12.95

HISS! POP! BOOM!
Celebrating Chinese New Year
By Tricia Morrissey;
Illustrations by Kong Lee
6 1/2 x 10 inches; 32 pages;
hardcover; color illustrations
ISBN 0-9715940-7-4
US$12.95

MY MOM IS A DRAGON
And My Dad Is a Boar
By Tricia Morrissey;
Calligraphy by Kong Lee
6 1/2 x 10 inches; 32 pages;
hardcover; color illustrations
ISBN 0-9715940-5-0
US$12.95

GANBATTE MEANS GO FOR IT!
Or...How to Become an English Teacher in Japan
by Celeste Heiter
5 1/2 x 8 1/2 inches; 158 pages;
paperback
ISBN 0-9715940-0-7
US$14.95

AMERICAN BOARDING SCHOOLS
Directory of U.S. Boarding Schools for International Students
Edited by Celeste Heiter
5 1/2 x 8 1/2 inches; 420 pages;
paperback
ISBN 0-9715940-4-X
US$14.95

THE SUSHI BOOK NEW!
by Celeste Heiter;
Photography by Marc Shultz
5 1/2 x 8 1/2 inches; 276 pages;
paperback
ISBN-10: 1-934159-00-X
ISBN-13: 978-1-934159-00-2
US$18.95